Foundations for the Future

GW00691587

University of Cambridge

Foundations for the Future – An Exhibition

Christie's, London, 5-25 January 1995

The University of Cambridge can claim to have made as great an impact on mankind as any institution in the world.

From Newton's discovery of gravity, Darwin's theory of evolution, and JJ Thomson's discovery of the electron, to twentieth-century breakthroughs including the splitting of the atom and the identification of DNA as the secret of life, scientific firsts at Cambridge have led to fundamental changes in the world as we know it.

Original thinkers from Cranmer and Erasmus to Russell, Moore, and Keynes have helped shape the way we live our lives, while Cambridge-based advances across the spectrum of medical endeavour have affected the quality of life for many.

Foundations for the Future, another first for an English University, is a major exhibition which looks to the past and to the future, reflecting on eight centuries of achievement while highlighting some of the cutting-edge research which keeps Cambridge at the forefront of academic success worldwide.

Embracing a wide range of subjects supported by artefacts and archive material, the exhibition provides a fresh insight into the University, its purpose and aims – not only its heritage, but the outstanding contribution it continues to make to the modern world.

Exhibition Steering and Organising Committees

Lord St John of Fawsley	Chairman, Steering Committee and Master, Emmanuel College	David Norman	Curator, Sedgwick Museum
		Onora O'Neill	Principal, Newnham College
Simon Jervis	Chairman, Organising Committee and Director, Fitzwilliam Museum	David Phillipson	Curator, Museum of Archaeology and Anthropology
John Deakin	Cavendish Laboratory		
Susan Fenton	Events Officer, Secretary to Steering and Sub Committees	Adrian du Plessis	Director, Reference Publishing, Cambridge University Press
Stephen Fleet	Registry	John Porteous	Bursar, Gonville and Caius College
Peter Jones	Librarian, King's College	Fred Ratcliffe	University Librarian
Bill Kirkman	University Public Relations Adviser	Lord Renfrew	Master, Jesus College
Peter Mathias	Master, Downing College	C W Squire	Development Director
David McKitterick	Librarian, Trinity College	Susannah Thomas	Press and Information Officer

Exhibition Designer: George Carter

Exhibition Project Administrator: Rosamond Allwood

Book Editor: Kevin Taylor

Book Designer: Geoff Staff

Picture Researcher: Jenny Jardine

Published by the Press Syndicate of the University of Cambridge
The Pitt Building, Trumpington Street, Cambridge CB2 1RP
40 West 20th Street, New York, NY 10011-4211
10 Stamford Road, Oakleigh, Victoria 3166, Australia

© University of Cambridge

First published in 1995

Printed in Great Britain at the University Press, Cambridge

A catalogue record for this book is available from the British Library

Library of Congress cataloguing in publication data applied for

ISBN 0 521 48367 0 paperback

Foundations for the Future

The University of Cambridge

General Editor

SIR JAMES HOLT DPhil HonDLitt FBA

Professor Emeritus of Medieval History;
Honorary Fellow of Emmanuel and Fitzwilliam Colleges

CAMBRIDGE
UNIVERSITY PRESS

Contents

PART I

University Culture: Past, Present, and Future

PART II

Cambridge by Subject

Message from the Chancellor

WINDSOR CASTLE

I suspect that even people with long experience of life in Cambridge may be a little hazy about some aspects of the University, so it would be quite reasonable to suppose that most outsiders would be baffled by the scope and variety of activities in the University.

This exhibition 'University of Cambridge: Foundations for the Future' shows some of the University's most significant achievements and it is on these firm foundations that Cambridge will base its plans for the future. The opportunities are there, all that is needed is the right calibre of people and the generosity of supporters.

Cambridge owes a great debt of gratitude to Sir Anthony Tennant, the Chairman of Christies, for inviting the University to stage this exhibition. I hope it will owe him an even greater debt when the Cambridge Foundation begins to see a return on this important investment.

Introduction

Sir David Williams QC MA LLB

Vice-Chancellor of the University of Cambridge and Rouse Ball Professor Emeritus of English
Law; Honorary Fellow of Emmanuel, Pembroke, and Wolfson Colleges

Foundations for the Future – this book, and the related exhibition – illustrates the
quality and diversity of work done at Cambridge. It shows how the University
has helped to create the modern world, and how it is itself now helping to change
and be changed by new discoveries. It sets out the University's plans to secure the
necessary human, material, and financial resources to maintain the quality of its
contribution to the world community in the next century.

I am confident that the University's role remains pre-eminent in the expansion
of new knowledge and in equipping young minds to play their part in a rapidly
changing and increasingly global society. Recent British government reviews of
research quality have placed Cambridge at the top of British universities for
research achievement. We are widely seen as a leader among universities in
Europe, working to the highest international standards. In Cambridge, efficient
specialisation goes hand in hand with an interdisciplinary approach: individual
scholars or research teams benefit from easy access to colleagues in other fields.
This is made possible by the wide variety of subjects across the sciences and
humanities which are studied at Cambridge as part of a single intellectual and
human community. The collegiate nature of the University encourages this
interdisciplinary approach – essential for grappling with the complex problems
facing our world. The intellectual stimulus of having many and varied faculties
working in close proximity is reinforced by the human scale of the colleges which
comprise a variety of disciplines within their senior and junior membership.

The teaching role of Cambridge likewise rests on a partnership between the
University and the colleges. The University carries the basic teaching load and
provides the main infrastructure of lectures, laboratories, and – increasingly –
information technology. The colleges provide the small group tuition that is the
outstanding feature of our undergraduate teaching, as well as supporting young
scholars at the outset of their research careers.

All this comes at a price – and at a time when national policies for a welcome
expansion in higher education have been accompanied by new stringency in all
areas of government funding. We have responded by diversifying our sources of
financial support. The overwhelming majority of new capital projects over the
past five years have been financed not by the public purse but by our alumni, by
outstanding philanthropists, corporations, and major charitable foundations,
and by other non-governmental sources. Colleges have likewise invested many
millions raised from past and current benefactors and alumni to provide affordable accommodation and other facilities for students.

Thus, the University is engaged in a major development programme which will
match the opportunities of the new millennium. Some details of these plans are

given in the contributions by the University Registrary and Treasurer which follow. We have already sought and found willing partners in the wider community for the self-help we have always practised. As a result, 1995 sees the opening of the new buildings for the Judge Institute of Management Studies and the first ever purpose-built home for the Faculty of Law, the largest Law Faculty in the country. The last five years have also seen unprecedented expansion in purpose-built laboratories for the Biological Sciences and Clinical Medicine, and new buildings for the University Library and Mathematics. Other new buildings are in progress for Biochemistry, and plans for the arts, Engineering, the technologies, and Physical Sciences are in active preparation.

This process involves a series of critical decisions on priorities and the allocation of scarce resources of land, finance, and staff. An unprecedented building programme in recent years by colleges and University alike has to be carried forward in an architectural and environmental context of great sensitivity. The statutory planning authority has provisionally determined the shape of development for the City of Cambridge for the next ten years: the University will have to fit in with these requirements, while planning for the next 30 years.

The *Foundations for the Future* exhibition has been made possible by the support of colleges and University departments and by the generosity of Christie's in lending its premises. For all this help we are deeply grateful. The beauty and intrinsic interest of the objects displayed illustrate the intellectual achievements and international impact of the University and its potential for the future. They also demonstrate the awesome responsibility of the University and colleges for conserving so important a part of our national heritage. As one of the most successful communities of scholars and scientists in the world, the University is actively seeking willing partners to help extend this success into the next century. I hope that some of you who read this book or go to the exhibition will be moved to visit Cambridge too, and see for yourselves what is being done. I also hope that you will decide to join us in helping to deal with the challenges of the new millennium. You will be warmly welcomed.

PROFESSOR SIR DAVID WILLIAMS

PART I

UNIVERSITY CULTURE

Past, Present, and Future

Foundations and Founders
The Character of a Collegiate University

Christopher Brooke LittD FBA
Dixie Professor Emeritus of Ecclesiastical History; Fellow of Gonville and Caius College

FOUNDING THE UNIVERSITY

Cambridge is a federation of colleges, all wholly dependent on the University for degrees and laboratories and much else that makes them part of a great international academy – yet all independent cells also of education and learning, each one separately endowed. This independence was made possible by their founders and benefactors, and is preserved by the independent bodies of Fellows who run them.

The University was founded too; but strangely we cannot name its founders. In about 1209 masters from Oxford, fleeing from a crisis there, found asylum in Cambridge; and after a while the Bishop of Ely gave them protection and patronage. If we ask the question 'Why are there two ancient universities in England, Oxford and Cambridge, and no more?', the answer is that King Henry III willed it so, in a series of royal edicts starting in 1231.

THE EARLY COLLEGES

Here are the three types of our collegiate founders: the enterprising and dedicated academic within; the bishops and other folk of standing in the world; and the monarchs. Thus Hugh of Balsham, monk and Bishop of Ely in the late-thirteenth century, founded the first of our colleges, Peterhouse. It was probably a Bishop of Ely who inspired Edward II and Edward III to provide higher education for the boys of the chapel royal in the King's Hall, later converted into Trinity; it was William Bateman, Bishop of Norwich, who founded Trinity Hall in 1350; it was John Alcock, Bishop of Ely, who founded Jesus in 1496. In the 1330s and 1340s appeared the first women benefactors – Lady Elizabeth de Clare, foundress of Clare, and Mary Countess of Pembroke, foundress of Pembroke. Cambridge was still a small and poor relation of Oxford until the 1440s, when King Henry VI conceived the idea of King's College, first on a modest, then on a very grand scale. He cared much for education, but the centre of his scheme was a vast chapel – and prayers for himself and his family. He never had the resources to complete it, but at the turn of the century Henry VII was to revive his plans, finally achieved under Henry VIII.

The plans of distant benefactors would hardly have been conceived, and certainly not matured, without the enterprise and skill of local men. A unique case was Corpus Christi

Lady Margaret Beaufort, foundress of Christ's (1505) and St John's (1511). Portrait in St John's College by Rowland Lockey, presented in 1598.

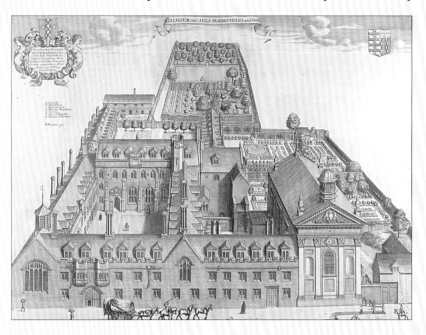

Pembroke College, founded 1347. From David Loggan's print of c.1690.

College, founded in 1352 by two guilds of townsfolk. Beside King's grew up Queens', under the patronage of Henry VI's young bride, Margaret of Anjou – but reflecting the imagination and persistence of Andrew Doket, a local rector and doubtless an academic. The red brick of Queens', later to adorn St John's and St Catharine's, is a signature tune of Cambridge architecture, which we owe to Doket and Queen Margaret.

John Fisher, Bishop of Rochester, Chancellor of the University, and patron of scholarship in Tudor Cambridge. Drawing by Hans Holbein.

RENAISSANCE CAMBRIDGE

In the 1490s came the meeting of two of the greatest of all the founders of Cambridge, St John Fisher and the Lady Margaret Beaufort, mother of Henry VII. From this friendship sprang the Lady Margaret's Chair of Divinity and her Preachership – and the colleges of Christ's and St John's. They bear upon them the stamp both of the Lady Margaret and of Fisher, the Cambridge don, who brought Erasmus to Queens'; and John's could never have struggled into life but for Fisher's anxious care after her death. In the 1530s Henry VIII dissolved the monasteries; in the 1540s he and his courtiers cast eyes on chantries and colleges. Under the guidance of a group of scholars, Henry VIII – instead of dissolving the colleges – founded Trinity out of three earlier foundations, added lavishly to its endowment, and helped to support five Regius Professors besides.

This kind of alliance between the man of vision within and the imaginative benefactor without has been a common pattern. Sometimes the two have been combined, as with John Caius, London physician and ex-Fellow of Gonville Hall, who converted his college into Gonville and Caius, and became its Master.

FROM 1600 TO 1870

The reign of Elizabeth I culminated in the foundations of Emmanuel and Sidney Sussex; between 1600 and 1800 – for all the fame of Isaac Newton and Richard Bentley, and the noble buildings of Wren and Gibbs – Downing alone was founded. In the years around 1870 the women students of Girton and Newnham first appeared: from the 1880s they made their mark in exams, though not as full members of the University until 1948. In 1870 the first of the great laboratories was funded by the Chancellor, William Cavendish, Duke of Devonshire.

Queen Elizabeth I, on the 'letters patent' issued to Sir Walter Mildmay in 1584 for the foundation of Emmanuel College. The miniature portrait of the Queen has been authoritatively attributed to Nicholas Hilliard.

THE TWENTIETH CENTURY

The early-twentieth century, with the coming of substantial government aid from the 1920s on, saw an immense expansion of the University sector – laboratories, museums, libraries, faculties – to rival the federation of colleges. Thus the genius of Sir Frederick Gowland Hopkins in Biochemistry was reflected in the great endowment by Sir William Dunn; and the Rockefeller Foundation, carefully steered by Sir Hugh Anderson, Master of Caius, endowed many of the human sciences – and gave half the cost of the new University Library, the largest open-access library in Europe.

FROM THE 1960S

And so Cambridge came to be a major international centre for the study of both sciences and humanities. In the 1950s and '60s staff and students rapidly expanded. There had been new colleges in the late-nineteenth century – Girton, Newnham, Selwyn – but the rapid increase came between 1950 and 1980. For women alone came New Hall and Lucy Cavendish – and the women's role was also much enlarged by their entry into all the men's colleges in the 1970s and '80s. In the '50s came Churchill College, a monument to Winston; in the '60s the University founded University College and endowment by the Wolfson Foundation converted it into Wolfson; three colleges (Trinity, St John's, and Caius) founded the new Darwin; and Clare College alone gave birth to Clare Hall. Wolfson, Darwin, and Clare Hall were to provide for the rapidly growing numbers of University staff, graduate students, and overseas visitors. A series of conversions has made colleges of Fitzwilliam, formerly for non-collegiate students; Hughes Hall and Homerton, colleges of education; St Edmund's, formerly a house of study for Catholics; and this remarkable movement has culminated in Robinson College, funded by a single notable benefactor, Sir David Robinson, in league with a group of leading Cambridge dons. The University sector has grown enormously; but Cambridge is still a federation of colleges.

Cambridge and Humanism

Patrick Collinson CBE FBA
Regius Professor of Modern History; Fellow of Trinity College

BELOW The Gate of Honour, Gonville and Caius College: part of the symbolic scheme of gates – also including those of Humility and Virtue – designed by John Caius for the college he refounded in 1557. Oil painting by William Nicholson, 1924, given to the Fitzwilliam Museum in the same year.

UNDER Coin bronze with a portrait of Erasmus, attributed to Quintin Metsys, 1519.

'Humanism' has distracting resonances for the twentieth century, when 'humanists' are understood to be thoughtful people who manage without religion. In early-sixteenth-century Cambridge, as, it must be admitted, in Oxford, a humanist was a student and teacher of humane or 'good' letters, and as a matter of course an orthodox Christian. Humanists were devoted to classical literature, and looked back to the civilisation and values of that lost world as a resource for the renewal of their own society, the process of 'renaissance'. These ideals and strategies were not as novel as the men of the Renaissance liked to think. But access to the ancient texts, especially in Greek and even Hebrew, was now more direct, and the new information technology of print made standardised and readily collated editions available which could be concentrated in larger libraries. Cambridge became a collegiate university designed primarily for the new syllabus, and dominated by those impressive and almost self-contained citadels of good letters: Christ's, St John's, Trinity, dwarfing and diminishing the 'Schools' of the University.

'Renaissance' nowadays means art and architecture. But while there was, eventually, an English Renaissance in that sense (anticipated in Cambridge by those remarkable gates which Dr Caius devised for his college), the more immediate impact of the Renaissance in England was in and through language and literature. The rhetoric, politics, and history of the classical world had a profound impact on politics, as not only clerics but future politicians were exposed to these studies.

SCHOLARSHIP AND THE AGE OF ERASMUS
The effect on religion was, if anything, even more pronounced. The availability of ancient Christian texts in their original 'tongues', the Bible especially, created the illusion that the Church could be restored to its pristine, 'primitive' condition; and that Jesus of Nazareth as depicted in the pages of the New Testament was somehow a more accessible figure than he had ever been in the flesh. Such was the humanistic conceit of the prince of humanists, Desiderius Erasmus, who taught in Cambridge for three of the early years of Henry VIII, expressed in his 'Paraclesis' or Preface to the New Testament, now printed for the first time in the original Greek, accompanied by a new and elegant Latin translation.

Erasmus was as responsible as anyone for the idea that learning of this kind turned its back on 'scholasticism' and the immediate past, giving us our notion of the 'Middle Ages'. Certainly there were tensions between the old and the new, and humanism of the kind personified by Erasmus helped to provoke that parting of the religious ways which we call the Reformation. But Erasmus himself was one of many early-sixteenth-century humanists who resisted Martin Luther and remained loyal to the old religion. Equally loyal was Erasmus's exact contemporary and the architect of early modern Cambridge, John Fisher, as much scholastic as humanist. Together with his great patron Lady Margaret Beaufort, Fisher founded Christ's and St John's, but died on the scaffold resisting to the death the 'Reformation' of Lady Margaret's grandson, Henry VIII.

PROTESTANTISM AND THOMAS CRANMER

It was not Henry's intention that his Reformation should make England a protestant Church and nation. But that is what eventually happened, after a protracted historical process, full of internal contradictions. In Cambridge these included the burning of the dead bones of the first protestant Regius Professor of Divinity, the German Martin Bucer, and then, four years later, his rehabilitation, the same Vice-Chancellor presiding on both occasions. Those who made England protestant were humanists in their formation, like William Tyndale, an Oxford man who may have also studied at Cambridge. Whereas Erasmus had written that it would be nice if ordinary people could read the Bible, Tyndale made that possible. His New Testament (1525), incorporated in a series of English Bibles from 1535 to 1611, is arguably the most influential work of English literature.

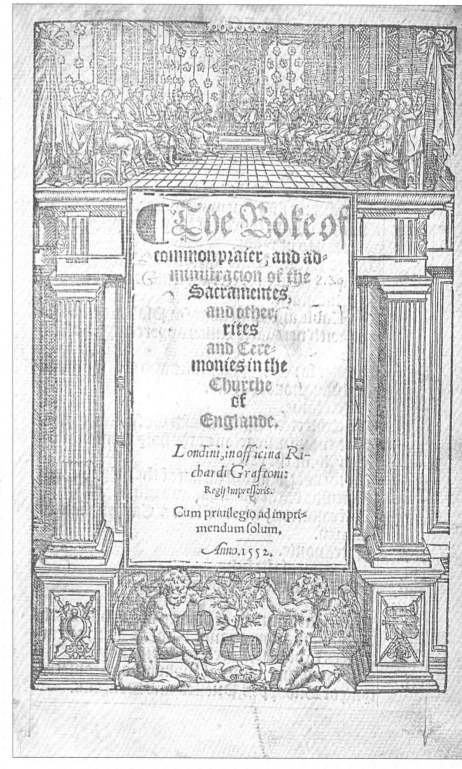

Title-page of Cranmer's **Book of Common Prayer**, 1552.

Thomas Cranmer, who spent 30 undistinguished years as a Cambridge don, was by contrast one of the Reformation's internal contradictions. He retained conservative views well into middle age and became a Protestant by degrees, assisted by events in the wider world of politics, which found him, at the age of forty-four, Archbishop of Canterbury and married to a German protestant wife. His martyrdom was preceded by the contradiction of a series of recantations, themselves recanted. Nevertheless, the moderate Protestantism of his Prayer Book, constructed with a creativity which was more synthetic than creative, formed the prayers and the conceptual religious language of generations of Englishmen to come.

THE INFLUENCE OF CAMBRIDGE HUMANISM

A full century after Cranmer went up to Jesus College, Cambridge was a fiercely orthodox protestant university. One of the newest and soon to be the largest of its colleges, Emmanuel, was committed to 'good letters', but only as a means to the end of sending out into the Church and, presently, to America 'godly' preachers and magistrates, some of whom founded Harvard. But it was not possible to limit or predict the effect of humane studies. Soon, out of the soil of Emmanuel itself, there grew the more reasonable, tolerant, and (to us) congenial religious system of the Cambridge Platonists, which it is tempting, if historically somewhat dubious, to see as the true legacy of the Christian humanism of the Cambridge of Erasmus, Fisher, and Cranmer.

University Libraries and Museums

Peter Mathias CBE FBA DLitt
Master of Downing College

The Vice-Chancellor's Cup: silver gilt, 1592-3, from the Fitzwilliam Museum. The Cup was given to the University by Robert Devereux, second Earl of Essex, who entered Trinity College in 1577 and in c.1597 became Earl Marshall of England.

The *Foundations for the Future* exhibition provides ample evidence of the richness of Cambridge libraries and museums; but Cambridge's treasures are not confined to these formal collections. Colleges and the University as a whole are treasure-houses and jewel-boxes of precious things and noble buildings – art collections (not portraits alone: witness the great Rubens in King's Chapel, or the Duncan Grant collection in St Catharine's); great silver; notable furniture (Christopher Wren designed bookcases, stools, and tables for Trinity, as well as its library); distinguished gardens. The most precious books and manuscripts are in the libraries – these treasures were identified in college statutes for safe-keeping from the fourteenth century onwards – but the museums are far from monopolising other collections. The treasures of Cambridge have accumulated as part of the wider national cultural heritage, by a combination of wealth, continuity, and good taste. Like the great private families in their mansions, the Cambridge colleges have consciously collected and preserved valuable objects over the centuries.

LIBRARIES

All federal systems are complicated to operate and difficult to understand. This is true of Cambridge libraries even more than of Cambridge museums, and not just because there are many more of them. College libraries – as collections of books if not as specialised buildings – are coeval with the colleges themselves. The first recorded chaplain-librarian of the University was in office by 1278 – the first anywhere in Europe – and the University Library was established as a collection of books in the fourteenth century: it has occupied its own building for more than 500 years. All Cambridge colleges without exception have libraries – which are among the principal attributes of a college as an academic institution – and now also most faculties, departments, and laboratories, in addition to the University Library. The Fitzwilliam Museum also has a notable collection of rare books, medieval manuscripts, and music autographs donated, with his art collection and an endowment for a building, by the founder Richard, Seventh Viscount Fitzwilliam of Merrion, in 1815.

COLLEGE LIBRARIES

Although some college statutes are silent on the topic, many of the earliest (such as those of Peterhouse in 1344) prescribe detailed rules for the safekeeping of books and manuscripts, with double locks, chainings, ferocious provisions against alienation or lending beyond the college, and termly audits. Theology and Law (Civil and Canon) dominate these early collections, but the sciences ('Natural Philosophy'), Medicine, Music, Astronomy, Alchemy, Geometry, Logic, History, Poetry, Metaphysics, Grammar, and Moral Philosophy are also present. Most great collections of manuscripts and rare books in college libraries came from benefactions rather than purchases, as with the University Library holdings and those of the Fitzwilliam. Archbishop Parker's gifts for Corpus and the University Library, Pepys's library for Magdalene in 1702 (antedated by the building which housed it), and George I's gift of Bishop Moore's library to the University in 1715, are notable instances from a continuing succession. The latest massive acquisiton for the University Library is that of the Royal Commonwealth Society library of over 350,000 books and 70,000 photographs, for which c.£3.6m was raised by appeal.

LIBRARY BUILDINGS

Libraries are buildings as well as collections of books, and many in Cambridge, old and new, deserve mention. Those of Queens' and Jesus are pre-Reformation; Peterhouse (planned by Dr Perne in 1588) and Trinity Hall date from the late-sixteenth century; St John's, Clare, and Trinity from the seventeenth century. Some were originally chapel buildings. All the early libraries were on upper floors, to protect the books against damp or flood, this tradition still being embodied in Wren's great library for Trinity (1676-95) with its open cloister. Pembroke and Emmanuel were the first libraries in Cambridge to be sited at ground level. One of the mysteries is why college libraries faced east-west up to the sixteenth century, north-south from then to the mid-seventeenth century, and indifferently thereafter.

These rooms are often now designated 'the old library' in colleges, because many new libraries have been built in modern times to cope with the great expansion of undergraduate numbers and the exponential growth of research publications (both books and periodicals). Some have proved notable – and/or controversial – buildings. Amongst the new college libraries of recent years are Clare (Sir Philip Dowson), Newnham (Joanna van Heyningen), Downing (Quinlan Terry, continuing the neo-classical aesthetic to which the college has been committed since its foundation in 1800), St John's (Colin Rice and Mark Beedle), and Jesus (Evans and Shalev) – recently commissioned. The History Faculty Library (1964-8; depicted on p.39) was designed by Sir James Stirling and has won notoriety from its users as well as praise from architects. A similarly avant-garde new law library (p.27) by Sir Norman Foster will shortly become its neighbour at Sidgwick Avenue. The University Library remained on the University's central site by the Senate-House from the fifteenth century to 1934, when the original medieval building (now the University Combination Room) and the later addition by C. R. Cockerell of 1837-42 (which subsequently housed the Seeley History Library and the Squire Law Library) were outgrown. Cambridge then – in contrast with Oxford – took the dramatic decision to build a great new library, designed by Sir Giles Gilbert Scott, on a green-field site to the west of the Cam, where space would allow progressive extensions (one major new addition being finished in 1993).

THE UNIVERSITY LIBRARY

The University Library stands at the head of an integrated library system in the University. The main library holds more than four million books and one million volumes of periodicals, with important special collections of manuscripts, incunabula, archives, and rare books.

ABOVE Interior of the College Library of Trinity Hall, c.1600.

BELOW Cambridge University Library: Giles Gilbert Scott's tower of 1934, seen beyond the Old Schools - where the first University Library premises opened in 1438.

It is the largest 'open-access' library in Europe and the one lending library among the five national copyright libraries with the right to receive (if claimed) a free copy of every new title and edition published in the UK. The main building is run by a staff of over 250. The University Library has three dependent libraries under its control on other sites – the Scientific Periodicals Library, the Medical Library, and the Squire Law Library – but, in addition, come the serried ranks of the departmental libraries, now more than 60. Some are ancient foundations: the Botany Library (1765), the Seeley Historical Library (1807), the Fitzwilliam Museum Library (1816), the Philosophical Library (1819), the Observatory Library (1824), and the Geology Library (1850) were the earliest. Over 40 have arrived since 1914, many in association with the growth of new scientific departments. With such a complex system, coordination, 'rationalisation' of purchasing, and establishing interactive databases become ever more pressing problems.

FACULTY AND DEPARTMENTAL MUSEUMS

The personal libraries of professors and benefactors explain the establishment of some departmental libraries, but others – such as Botany, Geology, and Anatomy – owed their foundation to the need to have a collection of books in association with a collection of artefacts for teaching and research. Thus, an intrinsic academic connection was forged between several University museums and departmental libraries. Paradoxically, this was not the case with the greatest and most famous of Cambridge museums – the Fitzwilliam – or with Kettle's Yard.

Mask in wood and pigment, from the Museum of Archaeology and Anthropology (collected in 1898 from Torres Strait and given by A. C. Haddon).

Seven of the nine University museums maintain the nexus between teaching and research, and therefore come within the faculty and departmental structure of the University. Although none has as widespread a public renown as the Fitzwilliam, each in its own special field has national and international status. The collections, while still accumulating, represent the heritage of previous centuries, whose replacement would be impossible. This is as true of many thousands of plant and zoological specimens as it is of the archaeological artefacts, the export of which would now be prohibited.

The Sedgwick Museum dates from 1728, when Dr John Woodward (a Professor of Medicine in London) gave his collection of fossils to the University. It has occupied its present building on the Downing Site since 1904. Currently over 1.2 million fossil specimens and several hundred thousand minerals and building stones are housed there, second in importance only to the collection in the Natural History Museum.

The same is true of the Herbarium Collection of *c*.500,000 pressed, dried, and mounted plant specimens, begun in 1761, with more than 100,000 plants of British flora. Apart from items made famous by the fact that they were collected by Darwin on the voyage of the *Beagle* (in common with many items in the Zoology Museum), the Herbarium's data bank has been given a new dimension of significance by the recent discovery that DNA can be recovered from preserved specimens. In certain respects the Herbarium must be seen as a collateral to the University Botanic Garden – another University treasure of international renown.

The Zoology Museum collection began in 1814 and became part of the new Zoology Building in 1968 – symbolising its continuing close links with undergraduate teaching and research. Internationally important ranges of primary type specimens in fossil vertebrates, insects, molluscs, fish, and birds (there are 35,000 bird-skins) are curated, including Charles Darwin's zoological specimens.

The Museum of Archaeology and Anthropology (1884) houses, with the Pitt Rivers Museum in Oxford, the most important ethnological collections in the country outside the British Museum. The range is worldwide (including material brought back from James Cook's voyages in the Pacific), with artefacts and over 50,000 field photographs and negatives. The archaeological collections also come from all parts of the world and in addition the Museum plays an active role in local archaeology: this is where *objets trouvés* are brought for identification.

Although its collections are more limited, the Museum of the Scott Polar Research Institute (1920) also holds a diverse range of artefacts, manuscripts, paintings, specimens, and photographs. Most of the items displayed are from Captain Scott's fatal expedition of 1912 to the South Pole (the Institute was founded in his memory) and the heroic age of

LEFT The Whipple Museum of the History of Science.

BELOW Students examine plaster replicas of ancient statues in the Museum of Classical Archaeology.

The cottage interior, Kettle's Yard.

British exploration in the Antarctic, but much other material originated from nineteenth-century expeditions to the Canadian Arctic, with Eskimo and Lappish exhibits in addition.

The Whipple Museum of the History of Science possesses one of the leading international collections of scientific instruments: the Museum was founded in 1944, based on the private collection of the head of the Cambridge Scientific Instrument Company, but now substantially augmented from the scientific departments of the University and by loans from the Fitzwilliam. Unique amongst its peers, the Whipple Collection is integrated with teaching, and also has an active programme of exhibitions.

Fine and applied arts are not quite monopolised by the Fitzwilliam and Kettle's Yard amongst University museums, because the Museum of Classical Archaeology has existed to fulfil a specialised role within the Classics Faculty since 1884 – being a collection of pottery sherds and vases, and of replicas and casts of some of the most famous sculptures of antiquity. It is one of the few large 'cast' collections to survive outside the Victoria and Albert.

All seven of these departmental museums are open to the public, attracting many visitors and fulfilling a popular role external to the University, as well as meeting their main 'internal' academic priorities. Kettle's Yard and the Fitzwilliam are distinct, catering more to a national and international public than to teaching or research needs. They serve, of course, as centres of research in their own right, by attracting scholars to the collections and by virtue of the research commitments of their distinguished staff. In the Hamilton Kerr Institute (founded in 1975) the Fitzwilliam has a specialised laboratory for training and research in the conservation of oil paintings, and there are specialised facilities in the Museum itself for the conservation of antiquities, prints, drawings, manuscripts, and books. But their main role is essentially different, and they are the museums by which Cambridge is principally known in the wider world. Even if widely divergent in scale and range, each complements the other.

KETTLE'S YARD

Kettle's Yard was given to the University, with an endowment, in 1966 by Jim Ede. His own collection of early-twentieth-century art, formed when he was at the Tate Gallery, remains as he placed it in the domestic setting of his cottage on Castle Hill – a unique period piece. To it was added an exhibition gallery designed by Sir Leslie Martin in 1969-70 and extended in 1994. Six or seven temporary exhibitions are held annually, supported by the Eastern Arts Board and other sources, together with an active education programme centred both on the house and the gallery. Jim Ede also created an endowment for weekly concerts. His heritage has been to make Kettle's Yard a lively centre for the contemporary arts in Cambridge.

THE FITZWILLIAM MUSEUM

It is impossible to describe the Fitzwilliam in a paragraph – the range and extent of its collections defy such compression. The only solution is to pay a visit. The grandeur of the buildings (the Founder's Building by George Basevi, C. R. Cockerell, and E. M. Barry, built from 1837 to 1875, sets the level of expectations, followed by a series of major subsequent additions) is matched by their contents. It is the grandest of art museums outside London. With 70 staff, the Museum costs *c.*£1.5m per annum to run – about half of which is provided directly from public funds at present; about a sixth from the University; and the remainder by endowment, the Fitzwilliam Museum Trust, and self-help ventures of different kinds – particularly Fitzwilliam Museum Enterprises Ltd, the commercial arm of the Museum. The Hamilton Kerr Institute is self-supporting.

With its purchasing budget vestigial in comparison with the flow of loans and donations (both for contents and for new galleries), the Museum benefits from great generosity, both indigenous – first and foremost its own Friends – and increasingly from overseas. It offers its own riches in return, as recognised by its *c.*300,000 annual visitors (two-thirds of whom come from beyond Cambridge). The collections range across all the main artistic fields, with Departments of Paintings, Drawings, and Prints; Antiquities; Applied Arts (including furniture, ceramics, glass, and silver); Coins and Medals; Manuscripts and Printed Books. One of the distinctive features of this Museum for the visitor is its civilised mingling in the galleries of paintings, sculpture, ceramics, furniture, and carpets. Scarcely a great artist of Britain and Western Europe is unrepresented. And – for the Fitzwilliam as for all the other University museums and galleries – admission is free.

The Founder's Building, Fitzwilliam Museum.

The Role of the University Press

Jeremy Mynott MA PhD
Managing Director of the Publishing Division of the University Press

ABOVE Richard Bentley (1662-1742), the great classical scholar (see p.40) who reorganised the University Press. His close editorial management of his own edition of Horace (1711) and of the revised edition of Newton's **Principia Mathematica** (1713) represented an important development. Portrait in St John's College by James Thornhill, 1710.

BELOW The title-page of the first book printed by the University Press (1584).

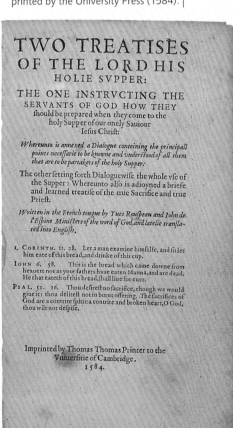

Cambridge University Press is the printing and publishing house of the University of Cambridge. It is an integral part of the University and has similar charitable objectives in advancing 'education, religion, learning, and research'. For centuries the Press has extended the research and teaching activities of the University by making available worldwide through its printing and publishing a remarkable range of academic and educational books, journals, examination papers, and Bibles. For millions of people around the globe the publications of the Press are the only link they ever have with the University of Cambridge.

ANCIENT AND MODERN

The Press is both very ancient and very modern. It is in fact the oldest printing and publishing house in the world. It was founded on a royal charter granted to the University by Henry VIII in 1534 and has been operating continuously as a printing and publishing business since the first Press book was printed in 1584. Since then, books under Cambridge University's imprint have appeared in each and every year, and its Press has grown to become one of the largest academic and educational publishers in the world, publishing some 1,500 books and 125 journals a year, which are sold to over 190 countries across the globe.

SOME FAMOUS BOOKS AND AUTHORS

The Press has over the years published works by many famous scholars associated with the University. Authors before 1800 included Henry More, John Milton, William Harvey, Richard Bentley, Isaac Newton, and Sir Thomas Browne. And from the late-nineteenth century the volume and range rapidly extended. In the sciences a tradition was established which leads from Clerk Maxwell, Rutherford, Eddington, Jeans, Einstein, Schrödinger, Dirac, and Bohr, through to such distinguished modern physicists as Hawking, Penrose, Feynman, and Weinberg. In the humanities there were Russell and Moore in Philosophy, Maitland and Acton in History; and the Press has in recent years published such internationally pre-eminent Cambridge figures as John Lyons in Linguistics, Jack Goody and Ernest Gellner in Anthropology, Quentin Skinner, Geoffrey Elton, and Steven Runciman in History, John Dunn, W. G. Runciman, and Anthony Giddens in Social and Political Theory, and Colin Renfrew in Archaeology.

The Press's journal publishing began in 1893 with the *Journal of Physiology*, which remains today one of its largest and most successful journals, alongside more recent productions like *Protein Science, Contemporary European History*, and *English Today*. In 1912 completion of the *Cambridge Modern History* inaugurated another distinctive Cambridge genre and there are now more than 25 Cambridge Histories published, as well as other large-scale multi-volume works like Needham's *Science and Civilisation in China* and the scholarly editions of D. H. Lawrence, Joseph Conrad, the Darwin Correspondence, and the Mathematical Papers of Isaac Newton. The Press's schoolbooks publishing began with the Pitt Press series in 1874 and has continued in this century to be associated with curriculum reform movements like the hugely successful *School Mathematics Project* at one end of the curriculum and the equally innovative *Cambridge Latin Course* at the other.

The story of the last 25 years is one of phenomenal growth and development. The range of publishing now covers virtually every educational subject seriously studied in the English-speaking world and has recently diversified to include reference works, professional books, Law, Medicine, software, and electronic publishing. The Press has developed one of the most important English Language Teaching programmes of any publisher, including major courses in

British English, American English, and Australian English. There is also a fast-expanding general reference programme, including the *Cambridge Encyclopedia* family of works edited by David Crystal. In all, there are over 12,000 books in print, along with maps, wallcharts, slides, cards, floppy disks, and CDs.

THE PRINTING HOUSE

The Printing Division has been through a correspondingly dramatic evolution in the last 150 years. In the 1850s, the University Press *was* predominantly a printing business, and primarily a printer of Bibles and prayer books. Now, the Press has a large modern Printing House with staff skilled in the newest computerised techniques; it has the first 8-unit colour printing machine in the UK; it handles every kind of work from traditional craft binding to electronic database management; and it produces a vast range of scholarly and educational books and journals, not only for the Press's Publishing Division but also for many other publishers and organisations throughout the world.

THE PRESS AS WORLD PUBLISHER

The Press is now in a real sense a 'world publisher'. English is the dominant world language of scholarship and science, and the Press seeks to attract the best authors and publish the best work in the English language worldwide; it currently has over 20,000 authors in 98 countries, including well over 6,000 in the USA (more than 1,000 in California alone), over 1,000 in Australia, and over 100 each in such countries as Japan, Switzerland, Israel, and Sweden. The Press itself publishes and distributes the whole of this varied output through its own network round the world: there are branches in the USA and Australia, each representing the whole list and contributing to it their own related publishing programmes commissioned from the editorial offices in New York, Stanford, and Melbourne; there are promotional offices in the major continental European centres, in the Middle East, Asia, Africa, and Latin America, with new offices being established most recently in Mexico, Italy, Poland, and Brazil; the Press is also pioneering a scheme to make its best textbooks available in special cheap editions for countries in the developing world, which will no doubt lead to a further expansion of the network.

THE FUTURE

The future will see more growth and diversity, as the Press develops a wider range of electronic publications, establishes a presence in new and emerging educational markets, responds to intellectual developments in the subject areas where it is already active, and continuously invests in technological change to improve its production, distribution, and information systems. But the whole of this great expansion remains essentially an organic development, purposefully and directly related to the Press's statutory aims, and realised through a unitary international printing and publishing organisation, with its physical and its constitutional centre in Cambridge.

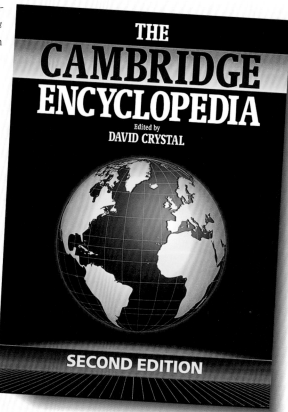

The Cambridge Encyclopedia, Second Edition, 1994.

The Edinburgh Building, headquarters of the Publishing Division of Cambridge University Press, whose other sites in Cambridge include the University Printing House, the Pitt Building, and the Press Bookshop at 1 Trinity Street (the oldest bookshop site in England).

The Work of the Local Examinations Syndicate

S. Tyrell Smith MA PhD

Deputy Secretary, University of Cambridge Local Examinations Syndicate

THE SCALE OF UCLES' OPERATION

The University of Cambridge Local Examinations Syndicate (UCLES) was founded in 1858 and is today a world leader in the field of educational assessment. Every year, over one million students enter for UCLES examinations in more than 130 countries. Over 60% of these candidates are from countries other than the United Kingdom.

Visitors to the Syndicate's headquarters in Cambridge are often surprised by the size and diversity of the organisation, which employs over 650 permanent staff. The examinations are run by specialist Subject Officers, together with a large number of highly skilled administrative and data processing staff. The Syndicate also employs its own printers, typesetters, designers, and illustrators to produce question papers and other documents. Another division arranges the distribution of eight million question papers and millions of other documents to addresses throughout the world. Some 12,000 examiners set, mark, and grade the examinations. These examiners are experienced teachers and lecturers, and their expertise and dedication are the basis of the extremely high quality, reliability, and academic standards of Cambridge examinations.

EXAMINATIONS IN BRITAIN

UCLES plays an important and influential part in the examination system in England and Wales, with a full range of subjects at *GCE A-level* and *AS*. Most *A-level* subjects are available overseas as international *A-level* and *Higher School Certificate* Examinations. As the Midland Examining Group, the Syndicate provides examinations for the *General Certificate of Secondary Education* (GCSE) and has been involved in the development of a new kind of GCSE examination for Key Stage 4 of the National Curriculum.

Cambridge vocational qualifications such as *Cambridge Information Technology* (CIT) are used in secondary and further education and by an increasing number of commercial bodies, to support the development of skills for the workplace. CIT is also proving popular outside the United Kingdom, with an especially high level of interest in South-East Asia and the People's Republic of China.

Pupils at Nottingham High School for Girls sitting Midland GCSE examinations produced by UCLES.

INTERNATIONAL EXAMINATIONS

In April 1992, Her Majesty the Queen conferred The Queen's Award for Export Achievement on the Syndicate, in recognition of the growth in, and quality of, its international work. The Syndicate is the only examination board ever to have received this prestigious award. Its success is based on a unique combination of academic standards and administrative efficiency.

UCLES has been involved with examinations outside the United Kingdom since 1863, when Cambridge exams were first taken in the West Indies. Today, it offers a complete range of international examinations and other educational assessment services. These are administered in Cambridge and can be used by schools and colleges anywhere in the world. Cambridge exams enable people all over the world, at all levels and all ages, to demonstrate their abilities to the full, and to receive proper recognition for their achievements.

Cambridge English as a Foreign Language (EFL) examinations provide a complete range of qualifications for teachers and learners of English and are internationally recognised as the standard for the assessment of English as a foreign language. Qualifications such as the *Cambridge First Certificate in English, Certificate in Advanced English*, and *Certificate of Proficiency in English* are a mainstay of English Language Teaching in over 130 countries, while the range of Cambridge Certificates and Diplomas for teachers of English as a foreign language are the most valuable professional qualifications for EFL teachers both in the UK and elsewhere in the world.

The *International General Certificate of Secondary Education*, used by schools and colleges in over 90 countries, and the new *Advanced International Certificate of Education* provide the international community with school-leaving and pre-university qualifications which are recognised by universities in many countries. Ministries of Education in Zimbabwe, Singapore, Mauritius, Namibia, and elsewhere use the Syndicate's services to provide *GCE O-* and *A-level, School Certificate, Higher School Certificate*, and other qualifications to their schools. These examinations combine academic rigour with an up-to-date approach to educational assessment. They provide some of the world's most widely recognised pre-university qualifications, with syllabuses in many subjects specifically tailored to the needs of particular countries and regions. The Syndicate has helped many countries to develop and set up their own examination systems and several Commonwealth countries are currently making use of this service. The help available ranges from the provision of consultants' reports to the installation of fully-fledged examining processing systems and academic support services.

As worldwide demand for internationally recognised qualifications continues to grow, especially in the field of English as *the* language of international communication, Cambridge examinations provide reliable standards for educational achievement throughout the world.

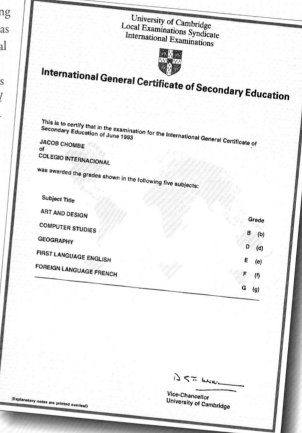

ABOVE An International GCSE certificate, signed by the Vice-Chancellor of the University of Cambridge.

LEFT Students receiving Cambridge EFL examination certificates.

Overseas Influence

Trevor Gardner CBE MA BLitt
Treasurer Emeritus of the University; Honorary Fellow of Darwin and Robinson Colleges and
Emeritus Fellow of Wolfson College

ABOVE The American Declaration of Independence, 4 July 1776, whose signatories include a number of Cambridge men.

BELOW Jawaharlal Nehru (1889-1964), Prime Minister of India and formerly a student at Trinity College.

Influence – the ability of a person or an institution to affect the belief or opinion of others – is difficult to confirm or quantify. This is particularly so in the case of a University whose teaching encourages objectivity and independence of thought. Cambridge has influenced development not only in education but in every area of life overseas; and an important part of this influence has been exercised vicariously through the former members of the University (of overseas origin or otherwise), working abroad in the professions, in politics, or in the arts. Throughout the world, Cambridge men and women are found in positions of influence and responsibility, and carry with them the memories and affections they formed as students. They are fortified not only by the knowledge they acquired at the University, where they were rigorously tested and taught to think with clarity and precision, but also by memories of their Cambridge experience which encompass much besides study. They are motivated by that experience, and by their loyalty to the University and above all to their particular colleges, which remain an enduring influence on the work they do.

FRIENDS ABROAD

Throughout the world, enthusiastic graduates participate in organisations which bring together Cambridge men and women to commemorate their University days and to organise support for the various activities of the University. Examples of such organisations are the American Friends of Cambridge University, which owes its success in great part to Gordon Williams, Honorary OBE (King's 1931), who presided over it for many years; and the Friends of Cambridge University in Hong Kong, the brainchild of David K. P. Li (Selwyn 1961), Honorary Doctor of Law of the University.

INFLUENCES THROUGH HISTORY

Cambridge men have spread their influence overseas at least since the seventeenth century, when John Harvard left Emmanuel for New England and helped found a new university at Cambridge, Massachusetts, which adopted the Cambridge collegiate model that would be followed much later by Yale. From that time, Cambridge men have influenced the development of overseas countries, sometimes by intention and sometimes by default – as in the case of Lord Cornwallis (Clare 1755) who, after performing a signal but involuntary service to America at Yorktown, went on as Governor General to give India a reformed administration and the enduring benefit of the Cornwallis code. Throughout the period of the Empire, Cambridge sent students as missionaries, doctors, agriculturists, engineers, educationists, and administrators to promote the development of what are now the countries of the Commonwealth. David Livingstone, returning from his missionary journeys in Africa, chose the Senate-House in 1858 as the place at which to deliver his most famous address, appealing to Britain and most particularly to the students of Cambridge to rally to the service of Africa.

It has been a two-way movement: increasingly students from the schools and new universities of the Empire were to come to Cambridge to study and to return home reinforced in knowledge and confidence to lead their own people – Jawaharlal Nehru (Trinity 1907), Muhammad Iqbal (Trinity 1910), Lee Kuan Yew (Fitzwilliam 1946), Rajiv Ghandi (Trinity 1962), and Tunku Abdul Rahman (St Catharine's 1922), among others. Cambridge in this way played its part in training those who were to become the leaders of the new Commonwealth.

FOUNDATION FOR FUTURE INFLUENCE

A guarantee that the historic influence of Cambridge will continue in the future is provided by a remarkable development of recent years. The Cambridge Livingstone Trust, established in 1980, has provided scholarships for students from Southern Africa (South Africa, Lesotho,

LEFT A ceremony to confer honorary degrees, 9 June 1994. The honorands include distinguished overseas visitors – the Archbishop of Armagh (Primate of All Ireland), President Richard von Weizsäcker, and Claudio Abbado.

ABOVE David K. P. Li, founder of the Friends of Cambridge University in Hong Kong.

Botswana, Namibia, Swaziland, Zimbabwe, Zambia, and Malawi) to come to Cambridge for postgraduate work; Prince Philip scholarships, established in 1982, have brought a succession of Hong Kong students to Cambridge for undergraduate study; and the much larger Cambridge Commonwealth Trust under the Chairmanship of HRH the Prince of Wales (Trinity) and under the brilliant direction of Dr Anil Seal (Trinity) has, since 1983, brought students from all countries of the Commonwealth to Cambridge for postgraduate studies, that Trust alone now supporting over 600 students. The Cambridge Overseas Trust, established in 1985 and now supporting about 250 students at the University, has provided similar opportunities for students from outside the Commonwealth – from America, China, and many other countries. Just as Rhodes scholars have carried the influence of Oxford to the countries from which they came and beyond, Cambridge Commonwealth and Overseas Trusts' scholars will carry the influence of Cambridge, but in greater numbers, to the very many countries from which they originated.

A MAGNET FOR SCHOLARS

Cambridge has served the world by its contributions to scholarship and in the welcome it has given to scholars from abroad coming to work here, as a place of refuge or research or both. Those scholars have enriched themselves and the University by sharing the opportunities that Cambridge has provided. From the time of Erasmus (Queens'), Cambridge has been a magnet for scholars from all parts of the world; and it has welcomed them particularly in times of persecution (as in the Nazi era). Men like Ernest Rutherford (Trinity) and Ludwig Wittgenstein (Trinity) appreciated the intellectual freedom they found here, as well as the opportunity to develop their work in discussion with men and women engaged in similar researches.

GREAT CAMBRIDGE FIGURES

My final word must concern those who have chosen to spend all or most of their working lives in Cambridge, but whose influence on the world at large has nevertheless been great. The list is long, including as it does many of the 70 graduands of the University who have won Nobel Prizes. It is necessary to be selective: I choose three men from very different fields whose impact and influence has been especially outstanding. George ('Dadie') Rylands (King's; depicted on p.21) inspired and trained generations of directors and actors including Derek Jacobi, Michael Redgrave, Daniel Massey, Peter Hall, Trevor Nunn, and Jonathan Miller – all Cambridge graduates whose impact on the world's theatre has been remarkable and will be enduring. Maynard Keynes (King's; p. 43) revolutionised the study of Economics and influenced, for good or ill, the development of the world's economy. Joseph Needham (Gonville and Caius) pioneered the study in the West of the development of science and civilisation in China, and more than any other man has contributed to the world's understanding of Chinese civilisation. To a major extent it is through the work of such remarkable men – and there are many of them – that the influence of Cambridge has been felt in the world at large.

The Role of Teaching

David Livesey MA PhD
Secretary General of the Faculties; Fellow of Emmanuel College

Whether it ever was the case that tourists wandered from college to college in Cambridge looking in vain for the University, today's visitors stepping off their tour buses onto the pavement at the corner of Drummer Street and Emmanuel Street tread on a manhole cover, which, as they would find if they were to stop and read, is labelled 'University'. Beneath pass the wires and fibre optic cables of the GRANTA Backbone Network that link together every college and University department, providing an electronic highway for teaching.

ANCIENT PARTNERSHIP

For almost 800 years teaching has been a partnership, between the various faculties and the colleges of the University. The image of the college supervision as one or two students led by a Fellow, and of the University lecture delivered in an unadorned lecture theatre to a hundred students, is a very small part of the story, past or present. College teaching developed, much later than University teaching, in the Tudor period, and by the eighteenth century dominated the partnership. This domination was to the disadvantage of the quality of teaching, just as the disappearance of the colleges from the University – such as has happened in Paris and elsewhere – would have been. The role of the University was restored by reform and by the evolution of knowledge, with the result that today's teaching excellence, whether in History or Computer Science, depends as much upon University as on college teaching.

SPECIAL RELATIONSHIP

Teaching is part of the spectrum of academic and educational activities of the University which embrace learning, research, and scholarship. These are interlinked, being both dependent upon each other and also benefiting from their mutual interaction. Advances in a particular piece of scholarship, or the progress of a research project, depend upon attracting young, able minds. Consequently, those committed to research are also keen to present stimulating and attractive teaching: teaching that is not only a passing-on of knowledge but also a means of stimulating and developing the subject through the recruitment of future scholars. Although it is the students who are taught by the teacher, both are part of the process of learning. Excellent teaching involves the teacher in learning, just as much as it does the student.

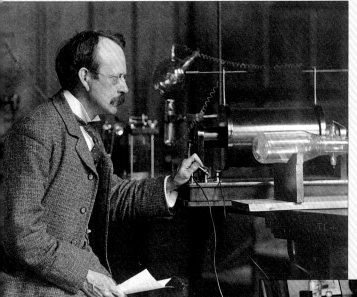

ABOVE J. J. Thomson (1856-1940) delivering a lecture in Cambridge on the Braun elm tube, 1890s.

RIGHT Helen Maud Cam, University Lecturer in History, giving a supervision to two students at Girton College, 1944. Four years later she would become the first female professor at Harvard University.

Constant reflection upon the knowledge to be conveyed, as well as upon the response of those being taught, inevitably develops fresh thoughts in the mind of the teacher.

THE STUDENT BODY

It is not only the nature of teaching which has evolved over the years, but also that of the student body. In the Middle Ages students were boys of fourteen or less. Today's students are not only several years older, but their origins, particularly geographic, are more wide-spread. They study a far wider variety of disciplines than the Arithmetic, Geometry, Music, and Astronomy which formed the Quadrivium of pre-Reformation Cambridge. Moreover, degrees are now awarded upon a series of written examinations which are more systematic than the oral disputations of former times.

THE MARCH OF PROGRESS

Although the teaching of the University has progressed over the centuries, it has not always been an upwards path, as its lethargic character in the eighteenth century testifies. Progress can also be slow, as is shown by the many decades which it took for the admission of women to the University to result in their being awarded degrees and, finally within the past 20 years, in their admission to the original male colleges. Innovation is not always progress. The external assessment of the quality of the teaching programme, the most recent innovation, brings not only the good news that the excellence of Cambridge's teaching is recognised, but also a potential loss of independence if the process were ever to be turned into inappropriate accountability to government for what is taught.

ABOVE Lecturer with overhead projec-tor: Malcolm S. Longair, Jacksonian Professor of Natural Philosophy at the Cavendish Laboratory.

TECHNOLOGICAL ADVANCE

The methodology of teaching in Cambridge has evolved as new technologies have widened the means of disseminating learning. The invention of printing significantly altered the way that subjects were taught and examined. Printing also generated the scholarly collections housed in University and college libraries. The University's organisation of practical classes in science and Medicine and, more recently, of language teach-ing facilities, has both altered the balance between college and University teaching and created the need for extensive University buildings.

BELOW Teaching in a practical con-text: Cambridge students with a mol-ecular beam epitaxy chamber, used to grow semiconductor crystals under very high vacuum.

Innovation has added to the repertoire rather than replaced older techniques. Lecture theatres retain their lecterns for the oral transmission of knowledge, whilst today's lecturer also has available not only blackboard and chalk but slide, overhead, film, and video projec-tors. The images projected may originate from a distant source, even another university, as do some of the medical procedures demonstrated in the Clinical School. The same information can be made available in college rooms, to assist with a supervision or as an aid to students' private study. All of this is made possible by the GRANTA Backbone Network. The optic fibres that form this Network also carry teaching material in many languages between the University's Language Centre and various departments and colleges. In the past, teaching was in the medium of the ancient classical languages, Latin and Greek. Today's students of Engineering or Law recognise the need to speak the languages of the European Union if they are to practise their chosen professions, and the University has responded, as it does in many other instances to changing circumstances, with appropriate innovations in its teaching, both in content and method.

Music and Theatre at Cambridge

Harry C. **Porter** MA PhD
Archivist of the University Footlights Dramatic Club and formerly University Lecturer in History

Theatre and Music in modern Cambridge combine variety and accomplishment. Some colleges have up-to-date theatres. College dramatic societies continue to build on distinguished reputations. The ADC (Amateur Dramatic Club) is now a University rather than a club theatre, housing University and college productions and visiting groups, as well as productions by the ADC itself. Once, King's College choir alone had a non-parochial reputation, but the LP and the CD have allowed many other college choirs to make their skills widely known. The chorus and orchestras of CUMS (Cambridge University Musical Society) and the University Chamber Choir and Orchestra have drawn on the National Youth Orchestra for their instrumentalists. The Concert Hall in West Road, opened in 1977 as the first stage of the Music Faculty complex, is used by gown, town, and guest performers.

MUSIC: PROMISE FULFILLED

The founding of CUMS (1843-44) was not the start of University attention to Music. There were famous musicians here in the sixteenth and seventeenth centuries, Orlando Gibbons (1583-1625) for one; and by the eighteenth century there were grand concerts on great University occasions: either in Great St Mary's (where in 1807 Lord Byron, Trinity freshman, heard *Messiah*) or, after its completion in 1730, the Senate-House. The University bestowed its first degree of Bachelor of Music in 1464. There was a Professor of Music from 1684; but the Professor did not need to reside, and until the 1860s was unpaid. For at least three centuries, the MusB was purely honorary; and thereafter available only to students who had already graduated in some other subject. There was no BA in Music until 1948.

The key figure in the development of University Music was Sir Charles Stanford of Trinity, BA 1874, conductor of CUMS, and Professor of Music from 1887 to 1924. For the 1893 CUMS jubilee he prompted the University to give honorary degrees in person (on the same day) to Saint-Saëns, Arrigo Boito, Max Bruch, and Tchaikovsky.

THEATRE: THE PHILISTINES RETREAT

Although there was a tradition of college plays – usually Latin comedies, but sometimes original satires in English – the academic establishment was traditionally opposed to dramatic ventures outside college walls. In 1855 a group of daring undergraduates rented rooms adjacent to the Jesus Lane/Park Street corner, and presented three one-act farces. Thus the ADC was born. In 1861 the undergraduate Prince of Wales attended two performances, and became an honorary member; later, as Edward VII, he was Patron. Establishment wrath was curbed. After a fire in 1933 the Park Street theatre was redesigned, opening again in 1935. Further improvements to stage and auditorium have been made recently.

Gown was also opposed to any commercial theatre in the town, but in 1882 a theatre opened between Emmanuel and the University Arms hotel. The canny

Music and entertainment in today's Cambridge: the Granta Singers perform on the Cam.

owner allowed his stage to be used by the University in 1882 for the first Greek Play – followed later in the 1880s by three further Greek Plays, two with music by Stanford. This theatre also saw, in June 1883, the first performances by the Footlights Dramatic Club. Thereafter (except in the War years), the Footlights have presented annual May Week entertainments, which since the early-1890s have consisted entirely of original material.

Another enterprising undergraduate group presented at the ADC two 'authentic' performances of Marlowe's *Dr Faustus* in November 1907. Thus the Marlowe Dramatic Society began, devoted to the presentation of Elizabethan and Jacobean plays in simple productions, with fidelity to the text and careful verse speaking. The Marlowe owes most to George Rylands (born 1902), Fellow of King's since 1927, who for over 25 years directed most of its productions, and acted in some. He also (1959-64) directed recordings for Argo of the complete Shakespeare canon, using past and present Marlowe Society members. The Society has had its musical excursions, combining with CUMS in three productions (1947-51) at the Arts Theatre of texts with music by Purcell. The Marlowe repertoire is not fossilised: recent productions include *Peer Gynt* and *Cyrano de Bergerac*.

BELOW The Arts Theatre programme for the production that launched the Theatre, February 1936. Margot Fonteyn is among the performers.

UNDER George ('Dadie') Rylands and Gillian Webb in the 1948 Marlowe Society production of John Webster's **The White Devil**.

THE ARTS THEATRE

The Cambridge Arts Theatre, financed by Maynard Keynes, opened in 1936. It is not a 'University' theatre, and its trustees and directors include representatives of the city and county. 'The Arts', however, has been home to many University societies: the Greek Play, the Marlowe, the Footlights, the Opera Society, the Gilbert and Sullivan Society. The Theatre closed in spring 1993 for extensive rebuilding. Other venues were found: the Foot--lights perform at the ADC; the Opera Society did Benjamin Britten's version of *The Beggar's Opera* in the West Road Concert Hall; the Gilbert and Sullivan Society presented *Patience* in the Corn Exchange; and the Marlowe played their promenade version of *Frankenstein* in the old sewage Pumping Station, now the Cambridge Museum of Technology. The target date for the reopening of the Arts Theatre is autumn 1995.

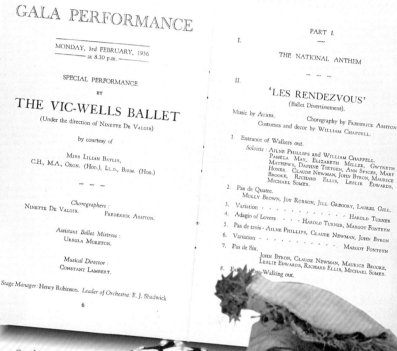

50 WELL-KNOWN POST-WAR ALUMNI OF CAMBRIDGE MUSIC AND THEATRE

Music: Richard Armstrong, Thurston Dart, Andrew Davis, Mark Elder, John Eliot Gardiner, Alexander Goehr, Christopher Hogwood, Robin Holloway, Raymond Leppard, Richard Marlow, David Munrow, Roger Norrington, Robin Orr, Robert Tear, David Willcocks.

ADC and Marlowe Society: John Barton, Howard Brenton, Margaret Drabble, Richard Eyre, Peter Hall, David Hare, Nicholas Hytner, Derek Jacobi, Ian McKellen, Sam Mendes, Trevor Nunn, Michael Pennington, David Pountney, Toby Robertson, Tilda Swinton.

Footlights: Douglas Adams, Clive Anderson, Leslie Bricusse, Eleanor Bron, Tim Brooke-Taylor, John Cleese, Peter Cook, David Frost, Stephen Fry, Germaine Greer, Eric Idle, Clive James, Hugh Laurie, Rory McGrath, Jonathan Miller, Jimmy Mulville, Griff Rhys Jones, Julian Slade, Tony Slattery, Emma Thompson.

University Sport

Anthony Lemons MA
Cambridge University Director of Physical Education and Secretary to the University Sports
Syndicate; Fellow of Hughes Hall

'The First University Boatrace, from Hambledon Lock to Henley Bridge, 10 June, 1829': drawings, based on contemporary sketches, which appeared in **The Queen, The Lady's Newspaper**, 26 March, 1887.

University sport is at once the activities of the University sports clubs, the sports clubs of the colleges, and the individual sportsmen and women of the University of Cambridge. It is a much valued aspect of University life, and has been so since the late-eighteenth/early-nineteenth century, when a lengthy walk or the equivalent horse ride were considered beneficial in promoting a good academic education. Around the world, the name of Cambridge University is synonymous with its major sporting occasions, and particularly those of the Boat Race and the Varsity Rugby Match which are broadcast internationally to an audience of millions. A rich heritage of sporting activity at the University is the foundation for the enormously diverse range of sports which is available to undergraduates today, through the 62 registered University clubs and the amalgamated sports clubs of the colleges.

GLORIOUS PAST AND GOLDEN FUTURE

Organised sport in the University is ancient, passionate, and remains a significant and important part of many, perhaps the majority, of students' lives. 23 sports clubs were founded before 1900, a further 16 before 1930, and four between 1931 and 1960, with the remainder being established between 1961 and 1993. From these clubs (whose members' ultimate achievement would be to win a Cambridge Blue by competing for the University against Oxford) has emerged a steady flow of distinguished international athletes, many of whom, on a voluntary basis, have continued to play prominent roles in the administration of their sport. The Cambridge sporting tradition, engendering a pioneering spirit and a concern for the future, is historically well founded. The majority of Cambridge clubs, established earlier than their national or international governing bodies, have had a considerable influence upon the development of their sport worldwide. There are few sports to the foundation and organisation of which Cambridge graduates have not made a significant contribution. The traditions continue today with current undergraduates and recent graduates gaining international honours in sports as diverse as Rugby Union Football, Rowing, Cricket, Orienteering, and Triathlon.

For most, sport at the University is concerned less with élite achievement and more with improved performance, attained through the development programmes of University clubs, the competitive intercollegiate sports programme, and increasingly by individual training programmes. The popularity, relevance, and importance of such activities have never been greater. Today's students need efficient time-management and require that University sport should truly provide *mens sana in corpore sano.*

SOME FAMOUS GRADUATES

Since the first cricket fixture against Oxford in 1827 and the first Boat Race two years later, Cambridge sport has produced many famous figures. Such legends of schoolboy dreams might include any of the following selection: G. O. Allen, H. W. ('Bunny') Austin, T. E. Bailey, C. Baillieu, C. Brasher, J. M. Brearley, M. Cox, T. G. R. Davies, E. R. Dexter,

P. H. Edmonds, H. Elliot, C. M. H. Gibson, M. Khan, P. B. H. May, D. L. Murray, N. W. D. Yardley, and D. S. Sheppard. The tradition continues today with current internationals including Mike Atherton, Rob Andrews, Rob Wainwright, Gavin Hastings, Mike Hall, Ian Morrison, Tony Underwood, and John Crawley. Dominated by men in the early years, women in sport at Cambridge have emerged more recently as a major force. The Cambridge University Women's Boat Club has produced stunning results (heading Oxford 58 to 24 overall), as well as triumphant national championship crews and several individual internationals. Our sportswomen are ably supported by such academic dons with enviable sporting credentials as ex-Women's European Triathlon champion Sarah Springman (University Lecturer in Engineering and Fellow of Magdalene College). Sport at Cambridge remains vibrant and healthy.

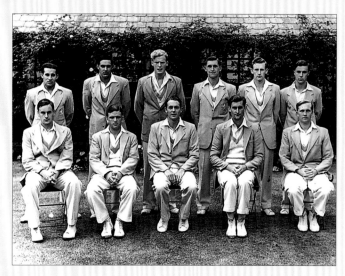

ABOVE The 1952 Cambridge cricket side captained by D. S. Sheppard, who sits in the centre. P. B. H. May, who went on to become one of the greatest ever English batsmen, is seated at left.

CENTRE Intercollegiate sport: the women's May Bumps on the River Cam, 1992.

BELOW Varsity netball: the Cambridge University women's team on its way to a 57-22 defeat of Oxford in 1993.

SPORTS FACILITIES AT CAMBRIDGE

With the acceptance of recreational sport and the development of competitive sport, many colleges had begun to acquire sports grounds by the latter part of the nineteenth century. These developments continued, until today most colleges have excellent provision for the traditional team games, for squash, and for rowing, with some also providing fitness training and limited indoor games facilities. In parallel, the sports clubs of the University were obtaining, by purchase or long-term rent (often with financial contributions from their members), more specialised sports grounds to suit their needs. Thus, facilities for Rackets, Real Tennis, and Athletics were all to be found in Cambridge by 1850. Later, the Goldie boathouse (Cambridge University Boat Club), Fenner's (Cambridge University Athletics Club and Cambridge University Cricket Club), and Grange Road Football Ground (Cambridge University Association Football Club and Cambridge University Rugby Union Football Club) were developed by those clubs under freehold ownership; while the Portugal Place Fives and Rackets Courts and Milton Road Athletics Track were held on long-term leases by their respective clubs. In 1948, the University built the gymnasium at Fenner's as part of the University Health Services, a clear reaffirmation of the recognition by the University of the benefit of sporting activity for student health.

LOOKING AHEAD

Since the McCrum Report of 1983, the University has been seeking to improve its sporting facilities, and the completion in 1994 of the new Wilberforce Road Athletics Track and Pavilion marks the first phase of this project. Subsequent phases are to include a University Swimming Pool, a substantial Indoor Sports Hall with training facilities and sports science and medical provision, indoor Tennis courts, and synthetic Hockey pitches, all to be built as funds become available.

The future will see growth and expansion in our facilities, academic research into sport and movement sciences, coaching, and medical sports services, as sport in the University responds to the increasingly sophisticated requirements of sportspeople. Health-related fitness will become an essential element in the education of students, the majority of whom are likely to pursue sedentary working lives. The advances in technology, information systems, and body function analysis will enable more efficient use of time (on the 'fitter faster' principle). The essential core to these major expansions will be the college and University sporting club structure, which will continue to develop and to provide those unique experiences that have been of invaluable benefit to so many of our undergraduates in the past.

The Cambridge Phenomenon
High-Technology Industry and the University

David Keeble MA PhD
Department of Geography and Centre for Business Research; Fellow of St Catharine's College

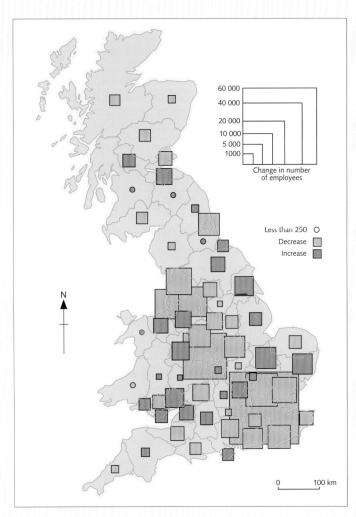

High-technology employment change in Britain, 1981-91. Map by David Keeble.

Since the early-1970s, the Cambridge region has become Britain's leading growth centre for high-technology industry. Betwen 1981 and 1991, employment in Cambridgeshire's high-technology firms, defined as covering a range of research-intensive activities such as electronics, computers, telecommunications, biotechnology, instrument and scientific engineering, and research and development consultancy, grew by 5,000 jobs or 32%, more than in any other county. Cambridge and its surrounding villages now house over 600 high-technology businesses employing 19,000 workers. Most of these firms are small and new enterprises, though some, such as Domino Printing Sciences, Cambridge Consultants, and Tadpole Technology, have grown substantially since their formation. Cambridge has also attracted high-technology investment from overseas, with major production or research units set up by Schlumberger and Napp Pharmaceuticals from the USA, Toshiba from Japan, and Olivetti from Italy. The rapid current growth of new, small biotechnology firms such as Chiroscience, Cantab Pharmaceuticals, and Cambridge Antibody Technology has attracted international attention, Cambridge being heralded by the UK BioIndustry Association as Europe's leading centre for biotechnology.

THE ROLE OF THE UNIVERSITY
The reasons for this remarkable localised growth are complex, and include wider changes such as the resurgence of small enterprises generally in Britain since 1970, and what many argue is an ongoing technological revolution based on radical innovations in computing, information technology, and biotechnology. Cambridge's location close to London and its international airports (especially Stansted), and historic engineering skills in radio and electronics manufacturing (Pye and Philips), have also been helpful. But the fundamental reason for this 'Cambridge Phenomenon' of high-technology small-firm growth is the presence and role of Cambridge University. This has operated in several ways.

First, scientific innovations developed by University researchers have provided an initial basis for spin-off companies, with major long-term effects. While the number of such companies has been relatively small – in 1984 only 17% of local high-technology enterprises were originally set up by researchers coming straight from the University – subsequent spin-offs from these companies have meant that "the University has indirectly been the ultimate origin of virtually all" Cambridge's indigenous technology-based firms, according to local economic consultants Segal Quince Wicksteed, whose 1985 report graphically charted this process of cumulative business growth. In addition, nearly half of all local high-technology firms report the existence of valuable research links with Cambridge University's scientific departments. Such links are epitomised by the presence on the Cambridge Science Park of Toshiba's Research Centre, whose Managing Director, Professor Michael Pepper, is also a Professor of Physics in the University and a Fellow of Trinity College. Firms on the St John's Innovation Park have access to advice from a network of St John's College Fellows, while the University's Institute of Biotechnology, which has itself spun-off three biotechnology businesses, maintains a range of research links with over a dozen local enterprises.

THE RECRUITMENT FACTOR

Local high-technology firms can also easily recruit graduate scientists and researchers, with over 2,000 science graduates and PhDs leaving the University each year. Thus, one recent study found that a third of locally-founded high-technology firms, and half of inward-moving businesses, reported 'recruitment of graduates from the University' as an important reason for their decision to settle in the area. The University's international scientific prestige and reputation also indirectly benefits local high-technology firms by conferring on them 'credibility by proximity', especially with foreign customers. Indeed, Chris Evans, founder of Chiroscience, Enzymatix, and Celsis, apparently decided to locate in Cambridge rather than Oxford in the mid-1980s because "Cambridge has that slight edge over Oxford as a birthplace of scientific excellence. That is what swung it".

INITIATIVES WITHIN A SPECIAL ENVIRONMENT

The presence of the University – its colleges, historic buildings, and cultural activities – also provides a residential environment which is very attractive to high-technology workers and entrepreneurs. Highly-qualified researchers are particularly choosy as to where they are prepared to live and work, and the historic and beautiful setting created by the University over centuries is a major reason for their readiness to set up businesses or move to work in Cambridge. But the University can look to the future as well as making capital out of its past, and an important growth-stimulating initiative has been the provision by colleges and the University of high-technology sites and premises, in the shape of Trinity College's Cambridge Science Park, St John's College's Innovation Park, and the University's High Cross Research Park and Old Addenbrooke's complex (where the Wellcome Foundation and Olivetti have established research facilities). The Science Park, established in 1973, is one of the most famous and successful sites of its kind in Britain, with 75 companies and nearly 3,500 jobs; while St John's Innovation Park, set up in 1987 deliberately to provide a 'nursery' for new technology-based firms, now houses 70 enterprises employing 5-600 workers. The continuing vitality and dynamism of the Cambridge Phenomenon thus reflects not only the unique research-intensive environment provided by the University, but also its direct support and encouragement.

ABOVE Aerial photograph taken two-and-a-half miles north of Cambridge city centre, where the A1309/A10 Ely road meets the A14 bypass. This sector has been developed since the 1970s, first with the Cambridge Science Park (occupying most of the centre of the picture) and more recently with the St John's Innovation Park (across the road to the right).

BELOW The front of St John's Innovation Centre (1987).

INSET Landscaping on the Science Park.

University Planning
Needs, Plans, Prospects

S. G. Fleet MA PhD
Registrary of the University; Fellow of Downing College

Cambridge is a university of international standing with a long tradition of excellence in teaching and research. It constitutes a vigorous academic community, based on a collegiate framework, in which the principal activities of teaching and research are strongly interactive and mutually supportive. Central to its success is its ability to attract staff and students of the highest quality. In order to maintain the attractiveness of its academic environment, and the excellence of its achievements, it must constantly update its buildings and facilities and extend the range of its work.

SOME FUTURE NEEDS

A number of departments, notably Engineering and Biochemistry, occupy not only out-dated, but widely separated buildings in which essential day-to-day dialogue between faculty members and their students cannot efficiently take place. Other faculties such as Law and English have never had their own buildings. Some, such as Mathematics, Materials Science, Divinity, Education, and Clinical Veterinary Medicine, are in inadequate and unsuitable accommodation dating from many years ago.

The requirements for new research and teaching of new disciplines point to the need for extensive further accommodation for Clinical Medicine and for Management Studies. Increasing pressure on space at the University Library indicates the need for a major new extension that will double its capacity from five to ten million volumes, accommodate new information technology, and incorporate a new lecture/exhibition centre. Additional space is also needed to improve the displays of the world-class museum collections at the Fitzwilliam Museum and the faculty museums and to provide more space for curatorial staff and conservational work.

In addition to building needs, the University has a particular responsibility to provide up-to-date facilities and equipment. These are increasingly sophisticated and expensive for the sciences and also nowadays for the social sciences, humanities, and the arts. A central modern development is the widespread need for computing and word-processing facilities: the installation of a University-wide computer network interlinking departments and colleges across the city (Project GRANTA), will enable study-rooms and, ultimately, many student bed-sitting rooms to be connected. The associated costs of computer hardware and software will be heavy. Among other equipment needs in Clinical Medicine, the Physical

Artist's drawing showing the restored nineteenth-century façade of Old Addenbrooke's Hospital, Trumpington Street, as it will look when incorporated into the new Judge Institute of Management Studies.

Sciences, and Technology are electron micro-scopes, mass spectrometers, NMR spectrometers, positron emission topography scanners, and cyclotrons. Another major new projected development to sustain world-class work in Astronomy is the construction of a four-metre telescope in Chile. Improved facilities in the Physical and Biological Sciences will depend on the refurbishment of Chemistry research laboratories to modern standards, and the renovation of laboratories in biological subjects (e.g. for genetic manipulative work).

The numbers of students in residence has expanded by 25% over the last ten years to a total of some 14,600, in response to the policy of the UK government to widen provision of higher education to greater numbers of the eighteen to twenty-one age-group and to mature and graduate students. This expansion has been accomplished without any loss of quality in the intake: indeed

standards have risen. However, there is a consequential and a serious need for more student accommodation to house the increased population of junior members. The colleges, which have done much in this direction in the last decade, badly need help for additional residential buildings, particularly for graduate students and married students.

Sporting facilities need to be enhanced to match the expectations of a modern international student community. The University has plans for a multi-purpose sports hall, a swimming pool of international standard, and an indoor tennis hall. There is also a need for further support of student drama, music, and the arts, including further modernisation and development of the ADC Theatre.

ABOVE Artist's impression of the new Law Faculty Building, by Sir Norman Foster: under construction on the University's Sidgwick Site, 1994.

RECENT DEVELOPMENT AND ACHIEVEMENTS

Against the background of needs and aspirations such as these, the Cambridge Foundation has been seeking funds since 1989 as part of a programme to raise £250m in ten years. More than half the total sum has already been raised from trusts, foundations, the world of

BELOW The newly constructed Isaac Newton Institute for Mathematical Sciences, opened in 1992 on Clarkson Road.

commerce and industry, individual well-wishers, and from within the University. Confident that further support will be forthcoming, the University is carrying forward development to meet many of the needs outlined.

Major new buildings for the Biological Sciences have recently been constructed on the Old Addenbrooke's Site; and others, including a Biochemistry complex, will start shortly. New buildings for Clinical Medicine have been completed on the New Addenbrooke's Hospital Site, providing for Medicinal Chemistry, for the MRC Cambridge Centre for Brain Repair, and for the Brain Imaging Centre. New buildings for Engineering, Materials Science, and Earth Sciences are planned, for construction on the West Cambridge Site alongside the Cavendish Laboratory. A major expansion of the Clinical School is planned at the New Addenbrooke's Site.

A new Law Faculty building incorporating the central Squire Law Library is in course of construction on the Sidgwick Avenue Site. Buildings for the Faculties of English, Criminology, and Divinity are being planned on the same site and its West Road boundary, together with additional space for Modern and Medieval Languages. The Judge Institute of Management Studies is being constructed behind the façade of the Old Addenbrooke's Hospital.

The Mathematics Department is currently in very cramped central accommodation, and plans for new buildings alongside the recently opened Isaac Newton Institute for Mathematical Sciencess in West Cambridge are being carried forward: these buildings should incorporate a new Mathematical Sciences library. A major refurbishment of the Veterinary School is projected, together with the construction of a new Equine Clinical Unit.

Building of additional student accommodation is

underway in a number of colleges, and also on a University site in Milton Road. A new eight-lane athletics track and sports pavilion opened off Grange Road in West Cambridge in summer 1994.

FORWARD LOOK: SIZE OF UNIVERSITY; ACADEMIC DEVELOPMENTS

In structuring its future objectives, the University envisages modest further expansion in the numbers of its students, of the order of 1% per annum over the next few years. Greater expansion than this is not considered sensible, since facilities are already fully stretched and the infrastructure of the city cannot cope with substantial further growth. The plans for new buildings and for improved facilities will go hand in hand with efforts to continue to attract world-class members of staff to lead academic departments of international standard in all major areas of study and research. At the same time the strengths that follow from full integration of teaching and research within the same academic departments will be preserved. The central role played by colleges in providing vigorous academic communities in which members at all levels, from the most junior undergraduates to the most senior professors, can interact and develop academic interests and strengths will continue to be fostered.

Efforts will be made to build further on recent achievements in widening the range of backgrounds of students admitted as undergraduates and postgraduates. At undergraduate level, more flexible systems encourage admission of persons of high ability from under-privileged backgrounds, as well as those attempting higher education as mature students. At postgraduate level, those with the highest aptitude, from whatever background, are encouraged to apply. The recent large increase in overseas students of outstanding ability (a doubling of number in the last ten years) will be carried further. Recruitment is encouraged by financial support in the form of grants and bursaries from the Cambridge Commonwealth Trust and the Cambridge Overseas Trust established by the University in the 1980s.

European links will be built upon and extended, providing financial support to enable students to spend time at European institutions as part of their course, fostering student exchanges, and facilitating the interchange of academic visitors.

A rapidly growing area of University work is that of Continuing Education. The University currently provides, through its Board of Continuing Education, a programme of courses which reaches about 11,500 part-time students each year. The University plans to develop this programme further and to attract more Continuing-Education students, particularly through the development of further award-bearing courses. This will also represent an important contribution in widening access to higher education for students who have not had the chance to go to university at the normal age.

STRENGTH THROUGH INTERACTIVE RESEARCH

In the field of research and technology, the University will aim to build on and extend its many existing interactions and collaborations with research units, and with industrial and commercial companies. These interactions have been greatly strengthened in recent years by the development of the Cambridge Science Park and St John's Innovation Park north of the city, and they continue to grow as many outside organisations are attracted to Cambridge. Notable examples are the Royal Greenwich Observatory, now located in Cambridge, the Laboratory of Molecular Biology (MRC), the British Antarctic Survey, and the European Bioinformatics Centre at nearby Hinxton Hall. Numbers of interdisciplinary research centres have been set up within the University in the recent past, notably centres working on superconductivity, polymer synthesis, and business research, all having particularly close links with industry. The income of the University from research contracts and grants from the UK Research Councils, trusts, foundations, government institutions, and industry has grown from £13.7m in 1982-3 to £63.7m in 1992-3. These interactions between the University and outside bodies make a major contribution to the national development of science and technology, and the University's involvement in such collaborations can be expected to develop and grow further in the years ahead.

In all these ways, the activities of the University will be expanded and enhanced to ensure that as the 800th anniversary of our founding is reached in 2009, and beyond, Cambridge University and its colleges will maintain a pre-eminent place in the world of scholarship, research, and advanced education.

OPPOSITE TOP Artist's sketch of the new Centre for Brain Repair on the Addenbrooke's Hospital Site, Hills Road.

OPPOSITE BELOW Colour study showing a bay, newly restored, on the front of the Judge Institute of Management Studies.

University and College Finance

Joanna Womack
University Treasurer; Fellow of Trinity Hall

The University chest. Containers of this kind were common in the medieval University and colleges, and were used to keep valuable objects secure. This one, made of iron, dates from the fifteenth century and survives in the Old Schools.

Cambridge is a collegiate University. The University and the colleges of Cambridge are interdependent and complementary. They are, however, and plan to remain, legally and financially distinct corporations.

THE UNIVERSITY

The University of Cambridge is a world-class institution at the leading edge of research, scholarship, and teaching. In 1992-3 it had an operating budget of approximately £209m. 60% of its income came from public sources, including grants from the Higher Education Funding Council for England, fees for home and EC students, and research grants from Research Councils and central government bodies. The remainder was derived from private-sector research contracts (from charities, industry, and commerce), fees for privately funded students, earned revenue, and endowment income.

The University's income is partly for teaching and partly for research. Under the former dual funding system, the University's block grant from the Funding Council covered the cost of teaching and administration and made provision towards the basic indirect costs of carrying out research (e.g. for laboratories, including technical support, computers, and library books and journals). Academic staff undertaking research projects applied to Research Councils

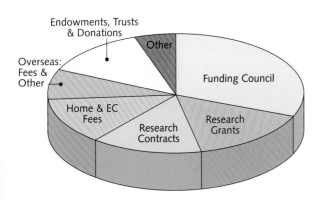

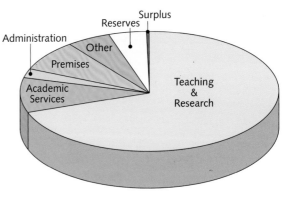

UNIVERSITY INCOME

Funding Council grant	£64.3m	(31%)
Research grants from Research Councils & government bodies	£32.9m	(16%)
Other Research Contracts	£30.8m	(15%)
Home and EC fees	£28.0m	(13%)
Overseas, fees, & other non-public-funded	£15.7m	(7%)
Income from endowments trust funds, special funds,& donations	£26.8m	(13%)
Other income	£10.4m	(5%)
	£208.9m	

UNIVERSITY EXPENDITURE

Teaching & Research	£144.9m	(69%)
Academic Services	£18.9m	(9%)
Administration	£5.8m	(3%)
Maintenance of premises	£17.2m	(8%)
Other	£11.9m	(6%)
Transfers to reserves	£9.5m	(5%)
Surplus	£0.7m	
	£208.9m	

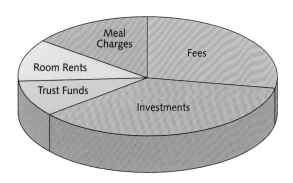

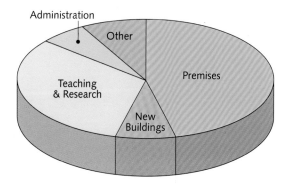

COLLEGE INCOME

Fees	£32.6m	(27.5%)
Income from investments	£43.0m	(36.3%)
Trust fund income	£11.5m	(9.7%)
Room rents, including conference income	£13.6m	(11.5%)
Meal charges, including conference meals	£17.7m	(15.0%)
	£118.4m	

COLLEGE EXPENDITURE

Premises and accommodation	46%
New buildings/major works	8%
Teaching and research, including tutorial care	32%
Administration	6%
Other, including hardship funds, admission, sports facilities, MCR/JCR, etc.	8%

for grants to cover the salaries of staff working specifically on those projects, together with other direct costs (e.g. for materials and equipment). However, over the past three years there have been significant changes in the way that scientific research is funded in universities. Under the new arrangements, although the Funding Council still pays for academic salaries and for premises and administration, the indirect costs related to specific research projects are all expected to be claimed from the Research Councils. More than £10m has been deducted from the block grant and paid to Research Councils instead. Academics have to win this back by applying for grants to cover all the direct costs of their research projects, plus a contribution towards indirect costs representing 40% of the cost of project-specific staffing. Unfortunately, although this transfer of resources was intended to be financially neutral in the university system as a whole, it has not so far proved to be neutral at Cambridge. The University's research funding has also suffered from the Funding Council's 'cap', whereby part of the increased grant which, on the basis of the Research Quality Assessment Exercise, Cambridge would have expected to receive, was withheld and redistributed within the University system as a whole.

The table and pie chart on p.30 (right-hand column) show an analysis of University expenditure. The University spends 95% of its income on teaching and research, the provision and upkeep of museums, libraries, computing and other services both central and departmental, the maintenance of about 150 buildings all over Cambridge, the provision of central staff and student facilities (careers, health, sport, etc.), catering, and on funding an increasingly over-worked administration. Most of the remaining 5% is transferred to reserves, including £6m (or 2.9%) for capital building projects, leaving a surplus after transfers of £0.7m in 1992-3.

By maximising income (shown in the left-hand column on p.30) and exercising tight control over expenditure the University maintains a fine balance in its finances. This has to be achieved in circumstances where the University's general reserves only amount to £24.3m and its accumulated uncommitted reserves, at £2.9m, represent less than 2% of its annual expenditure (or *5 days' expenditure*).

At the end of 1992-3 the University accounts showed accumulated endowments worth £334m. The vast majority of these belong to trusts and other special funds which can be used only for specific purposes. Only 11% of this total (£38m) might be regarded as 'free' capital. This amount is invested to produce income to assist with the University's regular running expenses. If all or part of this were realised for capital projects the University's income would fall, at a time when every penny is needed to support the enormously successful teaching and research programme. Nowadays, also, there is very little government money available for capital projects, such as building new laboratories or lecture theatres. This is why the current Development Appeal is so vital as a major source of funds for the planned capital programme for new buildings and to endow new teaching and research posts. In the period between 1978 and 1993 the University has spent more than £50m on new buildings, and projects worth nearly £30m are currently in course of construction. Large amounts of money have also been invested in new posts within the University, and on such items as student support, particularly for overseas students. These developments have depended very largely on benefactions: they could not have been afforded by the University out of its own resources.

THE COLLEGES

The collegiate dimension is provided by 31 independent colleges, whose finances are extremely diverse. The colleges fulfil major roles in admitting undergraduates, providing small-group teaching and pastoral care, housing the vast majority of undergraduates and many graduates, and maintaining college libraries, computing facilities, dining halls, chapels, common rooms, and a wide range of other social, cultural, and sporting amenities. College accounts are all published separately and are not consolidated in Cambridge. From published figures one can derive an estimated total income for 1992-3 of £118.4m, made up as shown in the table and pie chart on p.31 (left-hand column). A proportion (about 40%) of the college fees cover items which at other universities are funded out of the block grant. The value of these items (which include small-group teaching, associated office costs, admission costs, libraries, and Junior and Middle Common Rooms) is deducted from the University's block grant so as to ensure that there is no double counting.

Expenditure within colleges can be roughly broken down into the proportions shown in the table and pie chart on p.31 (right-hand column). The briefest walk across Cambridge through the colleges reveals the extraordinary extent of Cambridge's distinguished architectural heritage. Collegiate establishments are expensive, because of the high cost of maintaining historic buildings and of employing the skilled teachers needed to provide excellent small-group teaching within these academic communities. The colleges' support of postgraduate work is vital, with several hundred research studentships and over 200 research fellowships funded from college endowment income. The provision of housing, at affordable rents, is another essential area of college expenditure. More than 2,000 student rooms have been built by colleges in the period 1978 to 1993, at a cost in current-day figures of approximately £70m, none of which has fallen on public funds. The student body, both undergraduate and graduate, could not have been maintained and increased if colleges had not invested huge sums in building high-quality residential accommodation in the city. Further sums have been, and are still being, invested in student facilities such as libraries and computing centres. These developments, like those within the University, have been funded as a result of the generosity of benefactors over the years.

College resources, though substantial, are fully stretched. An idea of the scale of their endowments can be derived from the total college income from investments and trust funds. The spread is uneven, with a few better-endowed colleges holding by far the largest part of the total resource. Like the University, the colleges have generally benefited from major increases in value on UK and international stock markets over the past 20 years. However, their endowment income is essential to maintaining the collegiate structure and fabric which supports and underpins Cambridge's international reputation. As the government has imposed restrictions on the level of college fees, which have not kept pace with costs for several years, colleges have had to make increasing demands on their endowment income, as well as undertaking fund-raising and implementing financial retrenchment.

Philosophy

Thomas Baldwin MA PhD
Lecturer in Philosophy; Fellow of Clare College

Any account of Philosophy in Cambridge must emphasise the work of at least three men – Bertrand Russell, G. E. Moore, and Ludwig Wittgenstein. For these three, all Fellows of Trinity College, transformed the discipline of Philosophy during the first half of this century and made Cambridge the most important centre for philosophical research in the English-speaking world.

BERTRAND RUSSELL (1872-1970)
Russell came to Philosophy from Mathematics and his early work on the foundations of Mathematics led him to argue in *Principia Mathematica* (1910-13) that Mathematics is nothing but logic, although his famous paradox also shows that the connection between logic and Mathematics cannot be at all straightforward. In the course of this work Russell developed a new logical theory, and he used this theory to recommend to philosophers a new method of 'logical analysis' whereby, he hoped, it would be possible to resolve many of the traditional problems of Philosophy. His thought was that in a 'logically perfect language' – a language whose logical structure was transparent – it would be possible to transform the obscure tangles of traditional metaphysics into solvable scientific problems. Whatever one may now think of this, it was to prove an immensely influential idea.

G. E. MOORE (1873-1958)
In his famous book *Principia Ethica* (1903), Moore argued that because ethical disputes cannot be resolved by appeal to the natural and social sciences, we should acknowledge that ethical values constitute an irreducible dimension of reality. Moore further held that

The Moral Sciences Club, c.1910, including G. E. Moore (back row, left), Bertrand Russell (back row, second from right), and J. E. M. McTaggart (front row, right).

friendship and beauty are pre-eminent among these values, and thus that the best of lives is a life successfully dedicated to their enhancement. This message was taken to heart by Moore's friends among the Cambridge 'Apostles', such as Leonard Woolf, Clive Bell, and Maynard Keynes, and became characteristic of the 'Bloomsbury Group'. In later years Moore, who became Professor of Philosophy in 1925, turned his attention to the traditional issues of metaphysics and propounded a defence of 'common sense' against a variety of sceptical arguments.

Ludwig Wittgenstein (1889-1951)

Wittgenstein came to Cambridge from Vienna in 1911 to study with Russell. In his first great work, *Tractatus Logico-Philosophicus* (1921), he purified Russell's account of the role of logic in order to present an account of the limits of language which implies that problems of Philosophy are either such that they can be solved by logical analysis or else such that nothing can be said about them. Having, as he thought, finished Philosophy, Wittgenstein left Cambridge. But he returned in 1929, having decided that his previous emphasis on logical analysis had taken too much for granted, and throughout the 1930s he conducted his famous classes, which were attended by philosophers from all over the world. He brought together many of his reflections from these classes in his *Philosophical Investigations* (published in 1953), in which he seeks to pursue much further the questions about the limits of language that he had earlier raised, particularly in connection with questions concerning our understanding of ourselves.

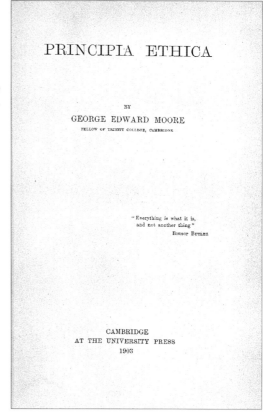

ABOVE The title-page of G. E. Moore's **Principia Ethica** (Cambridge University Press, 1903).

The Cambridge School and The Past

Several other important philosophers worked in Cambridge during the first half of the century, including J. E. M. McTaggart, C. D. Broad, Frank Ramsey, R. B. Braithwaite, and John Wisdom. This Cambridge School did not arise *ex nihilo*: Moore's ethical theory draws heavily on Henry Sidgwick's classic examination of utilitarianism, *The Methods of Ethics* (1874); and important contributions to logic had been made at the end of the nineteenth century by J. N. Keynes and J. Venn (famous for his diagrams). A little earlier, William Whewell's *The Philosophy of the Inductive Sciences founded upon their History* (1840) set the agenda for much subsequent work. In the seventeenth century, Christ's College was home for the 'Cambridge Platonists' Henry More and Ralph Cudworth, who revived Platonist doctrines of innate ideas in order to counter Hobbes' materialism and Descartes' dualism. But many Cambridge philosophers might prefer to look back to the author of the *Novum Organon*, Francis Bacon (who studied at Trinity College from 1573 until 1575), as the founder of their tradition.

BELOW Ludwig Wittgenstein (1889-1951) at Trinity College.

The Present

Several current members of the Faculty of Philosophy, and of the closely-allied Department of the History and Philosophy of Science, continue the Baconian tradition by reflecting on the issues that arise from the natural and social sciences, often starting from positions that owe much to the writings of Russell, Moore, and Wittgenstein. But the interests of Faculty members are probably more diverse now than ever before, including Feminism, Aesthetics, Political Philosophy, and Ancient Philosophy; it is symbolic of this diversity, combined with a reputation for excellence, that a major new *Encyclopedia of Philosophy* has its editorial base within the Faculty. The most recent change in the Faculty has been the enlargement of the postgraduate school, though this has made our lack of proper accommodation uncomfortably apparent.

Literature

Stefan Collini MA PhD FRHistS
Reader in Intellectual History and English Literature; Fellow of Clare Hall

GREAT WRITERS AT CAMBRIDGE

> At Trumpyngtoun, nat fer fro Cantebrigge,
> Ther gooth a brook, and over that a brigge ...

This is the opening of Chaucer's *Reeve's Tale*, a comic story which tells of how two Cambridge students outwitted a miller who stole their college's wheat. If this is Cambridge University's first link with English literature, it is certainly not the last, for Cambridge can boast a quite unrivalled roll-call of famous writers among its alumni, including Edmund Spenser, Christopher Marlowe, Ben Jonson, George Herbert, John Milton, Andrew Marvell, John Dryden, Laurence Sterne, Thomas Gray, William Wordsworth, S. T. Coleridge, Lord Byron, William Thackeray, Alfred Tennyson, and E. M. Forster. This proud tradition has been maintained in recent decades by, among others, novelists A. S. Byatt, Margaret Drabble, and J. G. Ballard, playwrights Howard Brenton and David Hare, and poets Ted Hughes, Thom Gunn, and Sylvia Plath.

LITERARY CAMBRIDGE

Of course, neither poets nor students are renowned for their restrained and orderly way of life, and the undergraduate years of those who were to become famous writers were often marked less by precocious literary achievement than by what one seventeenth-century observer deplored as "swearing, drinking, rioting, and hatred of all piety and virtue". At the same time, the enchantments of the place and the company of their talented contemporaries stirred the imaginations of these and many other writers who have spent some of their most impressionable years by the Cam.

Indeed, two of the finest poems in the language are elegies for college friends from Cambridge. John Milton was at Christ's from 1625-32, and it was for a memorial volume on the death of his friend Edward King in 1637 that Milton wrote 'Lycidas', recalling in pastoral terms their college days together. Two centuries later, Alfred, Lord Tennyson (Trinity 1827-31), was thrown into deep mourning by the early death in 1833 of his closest friend of undergraduate days, Arthur Hallam. Over the succeeding years Tennyson's grief at his friend's death slowly translated itself into his elegiac masterpiece *In Memoriam A.H.H.*, which was finally published in 1850. In section LXXXVII of the poem he tells of how he came back to visit Cambridge some years after Hallam's death, wandering about

> The same grey flats again, and felt
> The same, but not the same; and last
> Up that long walk of limes I past
> To see the rooms in which he dwelt.
>
> Another name was on the door ...

Other poets recorded less significant, and sometimes less affectionate, memories of their student days; perhaps some, like Wordsworth, experienced "a strangeness in the mind,/A feeling that I was not for that hour,/Nor for that place". Tantalisingly, one of the most famous poetic partnerships in history narrowly failed to begin at Cambridge: it was only some months after Wordsworth went down (from St John's) that Coleridge came up (to Jesus) in 1791. By contrast, Lord Byron's time at Trinity (1805-7) was characteristically extravagant

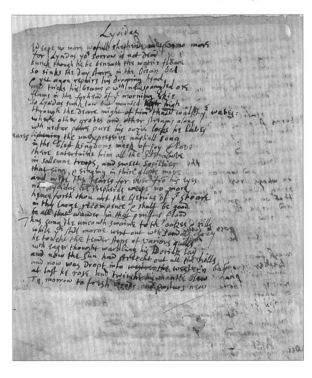

The closing lines of Milton's 'Lycidas' (1637), in the poet's hand. Manuscript in Trinity College Library.

and colourful; he delighted in vexing the college authorities, as when he came into residence at the beginning of his second year accompanied by his pet bear. Byron's scandalous life meant that when the memorial statue of him was completed it was refused admission to Westminster Abbey by the Dean, and now stands in the Wren Library.

In recent years, the most widely diffused images of Cambridge life have probably been of those dashing young men in boaters and elegant young ladies with parasols who populate the film versions of E. M. Forster's novels, several of which, such as *The Longest Journey* and *Maurice*, are partly set in Cambridge. And Rupert Brooke, an undergraduate at King's shortly before the First World War, author of 'The Old Vicarage, Grantchester', '1914', and other popular verse, has come to epitomise the glamour and narcissism of undergraduate life, so that Frances Cornford's lines on him have seemed to apply much more widely:

> A young Apollo, golden-haired
> Stands dreaming on the verge of strife,
> Magnificently unprepared
> For the long littleness of life.

ABOVE From a manuscript of a version of Tennyson's **In Memoriam A.H.H.**. This script, in the poet's hand, is dated 1842: the poem was published in 1850.

LEFT Life-size statue of Lord Byron by Danish sculptor Bertil Thorwaldsen, 1831, in Trinity College Library.

BELOW F. R. Leavis: portrait in Downing College by Peter Greenham, 1961. A distinctive style of literary and cultural criticism which influenced generations of students was developed by Leavis from the 1930s to the 1960s.

Cambridge friendships at the turn of the century also formed the nucleus of the Bloomsbury Group, which included such figures as Lytton Strachey, Maynard Keynes, Leonard Woolf, and Duncan Grant. But the most original writer of the group, Virginia Woolf, who did not go to university, did not always find Cambridge so welcoming to women, and she offered some telling observations on the exclusions and snobberies of the place in her brilliant feminist testament, *A Room of One's Own* (1929).

CAMBRIDGE ENGLISH

Before 1917, none of these famous writers could have read for a degree in English, since the English Tripos was established only in that year. But 'Cambridge English' soon came to exercise a decisive influence on the development of the discipline across the English-speaking world. Its early reputation rested principally on the work of a brilliant and original group of critics including I. A. Richards, F. R. Leavis, and William Empson. Of these, it was Leavis who became best known to a broader audience, in part for the sweep and ferocity of his cultural polemics, such as his scathing attack on C. P. Snow's *The Two Cultures*.

In recent decades the English Faculty's named Chairs have been occupied by such distinguished figures as C. S. Lewis, Muriel Bradbrook, L. C. Knights, Frank Kermode, Raymond Williams, Christopher Ricks, and Marilyn Butler. And the connections between critical and creative writing remain close: the teaching staff has long included well-known writers, such as J. H. Prynne and (until recently) Geoffrey Hill, two of the leading contemporary British poets, while several of the most promising younger novelists and poets have been Cambridge graduates. The Faculty's plans to develop its teaching and research into areas such as Commonwealth and International Literature in English, or Theatre, Film, and Television Studies, suggest that Cambridge will continue to be at the centre of both critical and creative developments as we move into the twenty-first century.

History

Sir Geoffrey Elton LittD FBA
Regius Emeritus Professor of Modern History; Fellow of Clare College

Some kinds of History had always been considered at Cambridge, especially in relation to Classics and Theology, and from 1724 the University had a Regius Professor for the subject; but History did not exist in its own right as a teaching and learning subject until the last quarter of the nineteenth century. Cambridge cannot take any credit for Macaulay the historian, nor need it accept blame for him. A Historical Tripos was at last set up in 1876, and quickly attracted a sufficient body of students.

The title-page of the first volume of **The Cambridge Modern History**, planned for the University Press by Lord Acton.

THE

CAMBRIDGE

MODERN HISTORY

PLANNED BY

THE LATE LORD ACTON LL.D.
REGIUS PROFESSOR OF MODERN HISTORY

EDITED BY

A. W. WARD LITT.D.
G. W. PROTHERO LITT.D.
STANLEY LEATHES M.A.

VOLUME I

THE RENAISSANCE

CAMBRIDGE
AT THE UNIVERSITY PRESS
1904

BEGINNINGS

The University was fortunate in its early practitioners. Though Sir John Seeley, Regius Professor when the Tripos began, has been commonly overrated, he did put a real effort into promoting the subject, and among the teachers of the first 30 years were some famous men. William Cunningham led the way in drawing his countrymen's attentions to Economic History; Mandell Creighton, who produced some interesting volumes on the late-medieval papacy, was also the first editor of the *English Historical Review*; and although Lord Acton virtually ceased to write when he took over the Regius Chair, he commanded much respect in wide circles. He also started the University Press on its career as the publisher of multi-volume, cooperative works of the history of this or that region, an enterprise which is still going on. But above all, that generation witnessed the arrival (and sadly premature departure) of F. W. Maitland, formally a Professor of Law but in fact to this day the outstanding figure in the medieval history of England and her law. Thus, once it had recognised them, Cambridge served historical studies seriously and laid remarkable foundations.

THE EARLY-TWENTIETH CENTURY

That work continued into the era between the World Wars, but it has to be recognised that the splendid beginnings settled down to somewhat ordinary routine. Certainly, a lot of undergraduates chose to read History: although the total number of University students just about trebled between *c.*1925 and *c.*1970, the number of them doing History remained much the same in that half-century. That is to say, History attracted especially those who (not without reason) regarded it as a softish option: studying which would enable them to enjoy the social side of the University. Of course, it also helped them to learn to think, and there were also some serious students of History, but the subject did not shine forth in its own right. It was widely held that Cambridge dominated in the Natural Sciences; eminence was assigned to the likes of Lord Rutherford and J. J. Thomson. In that era, Cambridge History was easily overshadowed by Oxford and also by London, places where the subject was distinguished by the presence of leading scholars and, especially at the latter institution, the prevalence of serious research. There were, of course, also important historians at Cambridge, but as a body they did not much attract the attention of the academic world at large. In a way, Cambridge History in that age cowered beneath the image of G. M. Trevelyan – a prolific enough historian indeed but one given to the search for literary and mental elegance, and neither a serious scholar nor, incidentally, much of a teacher. Perhaps this weak reputation by the side of Oxford represented a wrong bias, but wrong or not it was widely held. Despite the presence of medievalists like Zachary Brooke and David Knowles, of economic historians like Michael Postan, and of serious thinkers about their labours like Herbert Butterfield, Cambridge did not represent the first choice for anybody who wished to make a career in scholarship.

HISTORY AT CAMBRIDGE SINCE THE WAR

Things altered entirely from about 1950 onwards. History at Cambridge became a highly technical subject, demanding real work and thought, providing intensively for the teaching of graduate students (the next generation of scholars), extending its concerns over all the continents (especially India, Africa, and the USA), expanding into sociological and demographic enterprises, and setting the most rigorous of standards. Oddly enough, the move started with George Kitson Clark, a typical product of the earlier kind of historical study and in his younger days a competent but conventional teacher. He was forty-nine years old when he visited the United States for the first time, and there encountered both professional attitudes to the study of the past and the concept of a graduate school. On his return after a year's absence, he in effect began a second career, both in his own work and in his now ardent concern to train the next generation systematically. He specialised in nineteenth-century Britain, but by stages affected just about every branch of the discipline, with the setting-up of graduate seminars in most areas. Some traditional themes underwent real revolutions in the hands of scholars coming from abroad: thus Walter Ullmann gave a new face to the Middle Ages, and Sir Moses Finley developed the social history of Antiquity. From being a pleasant but somewhat amateur undertaking, History at Cambridge became a throbbing centre of advanced work and learning, and in consequence a training ground from which there soon emerged young scholars teaching the world over, including (somewhat surprisingly) at Oxford. In the end, that senior University even found itself looking to Cambridge for its Regius Professor.

Recent public assessments have left no doubt about this profound transformation. Maitland's principles of true scholarship at last took charge of the institution where he had first demonstrated them, and today, at Cambridge, History deservedly has the sort of central role and reputation which 50 years ago were reserved for the Natural Sciences. This transformation now runs through the subject at every stage. I personally have some doubts about the proliferation of limited topics investigated down to the roots at undergraduate level; this can deprive the student too easily of the important sense of continuity and coherence. But I respect the desire to treat even Tripos candidates as budding scholars, and I have no doubts at all about what has happened at the postgraduate stage. At present, scholars whose doctoral research was supervised here teach not only all over England, Scotland, and Ireland, but also in a good many American institutions as well as in Australia and New Zealand. Cambridge History has grown to impressive maturity.

ABOVE F. W. Maitland (1850-1906), the legal historian who stood out among his contemporaries in late-nineteenth-century Cambridge. Portrait by Beatrice Lock in Downing College.

BELOW Centre of modern operations: the History Faculty Building by James Stirling, 1964-8, on the Sidgwick Site.

Classics and Archaeology

James Diggle LittD FBA
Reader in Greek and Latin; Fellow of Queens' College

Anthony Snodgrass PhD FBA FSA
Laurence Professor of Classical Archaeology; Fellow of Clare College

and **Lord Renfrew of Kaimsthorn** ScD FBA FSA
Disney Professor of Archaeology, Director of the McDonald Institute for Archaeological Research; Master of Jesus College

CLASSICAL TEXTS

In the field of classical linguistic scholarship, the three greatest textual critics which any country has produced held Chairs in Cambridge: Richard Bentley (1662-1742; depicted on p.12), Richard Porson (1759-1808), and A. E. Housman (1859-1936) – the latter better known for his own poetry in English. Their legacy in this central field of classical scholarship is alive to this day: Porson's penetrating work on the texts of Greek tragic drama has been built on in the production, by recent Cambridge scholars, of the most reliable texts of each of the three great tragedians, Aeschylus, Sophocles, and Euripides, while Housman set new standards of rigour and exactness in the criticism and elucidation of the texts of Latin poetry.

Pride of place, however, is usually given to Richard Bentley. He was one of the most learned men of his age, with his own more than amateur knowledge of science and Mathematics (Newton was among his friends), and held for 42 years the Mastership of Trinity College. He was deeply embroiled in the fierce intellectual controversies of his time, and for this he was satirised by Pope and Swift. But his chief claim to lasting fame is the pioneering work which he did in the editing and interpretation of classical texts, especially those of the Latin poets Horace, Terence, and Manilius. His intellectual gifts and profound, unborrowed learning have inspired all later generations of scholars.

Cambridge has an unrivalled tradition of scholarship in the classical and archaeological fields. This inscribed Roman dedication-slab from Risingham (Northumbria), recorded in Camden's **Britannia** in the sixteenth century, is in the University's Museum of Archaeology and Anthropology.

THE CAMBRIDGE SCHOOL

But the scope of Classics has also been vastly enlarged since Bentley's day, and at almost every turn Cambridge has been at the forefront (most conspicuously in John Chadwick's contribution to the decipherment of the Bronze Age Linear B script in the 1950s). The phrase 'Cambridge School' was probably first heard at the beginning of this century, as applied to the circle of the pioneering anthropologist Jane Harrison and the philosopher F. M. Cornford. In the second half of the century, it has been revived in the context of the approach to Ancient Social and Economic History most closely associated with Sir Moses Finley (1912-1986); and more recently still in the field of Archaeology.

PREHISTORY AT CAMBRIDGE

Archaeology was first explicitly recognised at Cambridge in 1851 with the foundation of the Disney Chair, the first university Chair in the subject in the British Isles. It was not, however, until 1937 that growing interest in the field of Prehistory led for the first time to the appointment of an archaeological fieldworker and prehistorian to the Chair. This was Dorothy Garrod (1892-1968), who held distinction also as the first woman professor in Cambridge in any subject.

Dorothy Garrod was a pioneer in several ways: her principal fieldwork was in the Near East, in Iraq and Palestine. Her notable excavations at Mount Carmel supplied the key to a large section of the prehistory of this part of the Near East, notably in the palaeolithic (old stone age) period: in particular, they produced important human fossil remains which cast new light on the arrival of our own species, *Homo sapiens sapiens*, and on the still vexed question of its relationship with the fossil remains of Neanderthal

ABOVE Photographic portrait of Dorothy Garrod, Cambridge's first woman professor, by Ramsey and Muspratt, 1952.

man. Garrod also identified and investigated sites of the Natufian culture, the precursor of the earliest farming culture of the world, which subsequently developed in this area. Two great themes – human origins and farming origins – were notably advanced by her work.

Grahame Clark (born 1907: now Sir Grahame), her successor to the Disney Chair in 1952, followed and extended Garrod's interest in the interrelationship between humans and their environment with his investigation of the ecological approach, one of the early developments in the field of Archaeological Science, which has become a growth area in recent decades. His excavations at Star Carr, a waterlogged mesolithic site in Yorkshire, developed a whole range of environmental approaches, including pollen analysis.

ARCHAEOLOGICAL THEORY AND ARCHAEOLOGICAL SCIENCE

The other principal growth area is the lively interest in the field of Archaeological Theory. This was anticipated and encouraged by the next holder of the Disney Chair, Glyn Daniel (1914-1986), who succeeded Clark in 1974, and whose *A Hundred Years of Archaeology* was perhaps the first survey and history of Archaeology as a discipline. It was published in 1962, just prior to the developments in archaeological theory and practice often designated the New Archaeology, which were influential in the 1970s and 1980s.

BELOW The McDonald Institute for Archaeological Research at about the time of its opening in 1994.

These various strands in Archaeology have recently been furthered in Cambridge by the foundation in 1990 of the George Pitt-Rivers Chair of Archaeological Science, and in 1989 by the major benefaction from the late Dr D. M. McDonald. This has led to the foundation of the McDonald Institute for Archaeological Research, allowing the construction of major new buildings which have just been completed.

Archaeology at Cambridge has for most of this century been associated closely with Social Anthropology and with Biological Anthropology, as well as with Classics. Other branches of world Archaeology, including Egyptology, are supported within the Faculty of Oriental Studies. Most fall also within the scope of the collections of the University Museum of Archaeology and Anthropology, which has itself supported notable research in Africa, America, Australia, and the Pacific.

Economics and Business

G. C. Harcourt AO PhD LittD FASSA
Reader in the History of Economic Theory; Fellow of Jesus College

ABOVE Alfred Marshall: founding influence on Cambridge Economics. Portrait by William Rothenstein in St John's College.

BELOW Photographic portrait of Joan Robinson, a leading voice in Cambridge Economics who was described by John Kenneth Galbraith as the most diversely interesting economist of their generation, by Ramsay and Muspratt, in the Marshall Library of the Faculty of Economics and Politics.

THE MORAL APPROACH

One organising principle through which to understand the approach and achievements of Cambridge Economics is to see its main contributors as struggling with G. E. Moore's conundrum: is it possible both to be good and to do good? Though Alfred Marshall took the study of Economics from the Moral Sciences Tripos to be a Tripos in its own right in 1903, partly in order to create professional economists, its origin as a branch of Moral Philosophy never completely disappeared. Marshall fervently wished that Cambridge Economics would send into the world young men (he had reneged on the desirability of tertiary education for women soon after his marriage to Mary Paley Marshall) with "cool heads but warm hearts". (He also hoped his *Principles* would be read by businessmen.) Maynard Keynes wished economists to be humble and useful people like dentists, the trustees of the possibility of civilisation. Their role was to tame the forces of ignorance and uncertainty, in such a way as to allow people generally the opportunity to reach their potential, principally by ensuring that the most vulnerable were protected from the malfunctionings of our economic systems by discovering their causes and designing appropriate policies to reduce their effects.

This spirit inspired the successors of Marshall and Keynes in the Faculty – e.g. A. C. Pigou, Maurice Dobb, James Meade, Austin and Joan Robinson, Richard Kahn, Nicky Kaldor, Brian Reddaway, Richard Stone – in both their theoretical and applied work on advanced economies and, increasingly in the post-War years, on developing economies too. Moreover, when Frank Hahn, Kahn's successor, read Marshall's *Principles* in 1990 in order to write a paper to celebrate its centenary, he said how much he approved of Marshall's moral stance and how much he wished there could be more of it in modern Economics.

Marshall's approach to Economics – his organon – on which his pupils were brought up, was based on the dichotomy between the real and the money. Volume I of *Principles* was concerned with the operation of the real sector of the economy, independently of money and financial institutions generally. In it, the competitive normal prices of commodities and of the services of the factors of production were analyzed within his famous time periods – market, short and long – by his beloved supply and demand schedules. Volume II explained the general price level (through the infamous quantity theory of money) and the roles of money and financial institutions, taking the real sector as given and, at least in the long period, unaffected by monetary matters. Keynes spent much of his professional life working within this tradition, expositing and developing it, especially in analyses of short-term disturbances and applicable policies.

MAYNARD KEYNES AND CLASSICAL ECONOMICS

Keynes's revolutionary contribution, however, was to make an almost complete break from the tradition. He put in its place the theory of a monetary production economy in which money and financial matters were integrated right from the start of the analysis. This was the core of his *magnum opus, The General Theory of Employment, Interest and Money* (1936). Keynes was also an original and powerful philosopher and he wished Economics to remain a branch of Moral Philosophy. His philosophical views were reflected in his Economics in three ways. First, he argued that there was a spectrum of languages running from intuition and poetry through lawyer-like arguments to formal logic and Mathematics, all of which have appropriate roles to play in economic theorising. Secondly, his realisation, when writing what was to become *A Treatise on Probability* (1921), that the whole may be more than the sum of the parts, paved the way for the creation of modern Macroeconomics. Thirdly, his musings on how reasonable people behave in uncertain environments, and on the systemic effects of their behaviour, came to dominate his understanding of the malfunctioning of capitalism, especially why it was so often characterised by sustained levels of unemployment.

OTHER MODERN DEVELOPMENTS

Cambridge was also associated with another revolution in economic theory in the 1920s and 1930s – the theories of imperfect competition. They changed both the emphasis and approach of the theory of value and distribution. The principal contributors were Piero Sraffa, Richard Kahn, Joan Robinson, and Austin Robinson. Strangely, none of these economists, though they were closely associated, in different degrees, with the development and propagation of Keynes's new views, ever integrated the two developments. This was done first by Michal Kalecki (who independently discovered the main propositions of *The General Theory*) and Lorie Tarshis, and then (especially over the last 15-20 years or so) mainly by economists elsewhere.

Through Keynes and his followers, there grew up in the post-War years a robust approach to Economic History and to applied and policy work, principally through the Department of Applied Economics under its four Directors (to date) – Stone, Reddaway, Wynne Godley, and David Newbery – but also through the writings of Cambridge teaching officers as well: Phyllis Deane, Kaldor, Robin Matthews, and Meade, for example. The pre-War dominance in theory receded in the post-War years as Keynes' 'pupils' tried "to generalise *The General Theory* to the long period", only to feel in the end that their efforts had not been successful, that the attempt to link Keynesian, classical, and Marxian ideas together in growth models was not fruitful. Fortunately, the work on models of cyclical growth by Kalecki, Richard Goodwin (who spent 30 years at Cambridge), and their followers is now making headway in the discipline at large.

Even more than shedding light, Cambridge Economics has wished (it wishes still) to bear fruit – Pigou's aim in his classic writings on Welfare Economics. Of no-one was this more true than Keynes: witness, for example, his courageous and passionate attack on the Treaty of Versailles in *The Economic Consequences of the Peace* (1919) and, most of all, his heroic efforts during the Second World War. Though an extremely sick man, he not only made vital contributions to the Economics of the War effort but also helped to design the institutions and new rules of the game for the post-War world, so that unemployment would never again be a scourge (!) and the benefits of the international division of labour through freer trade and flow of capital funds could help to raise world living standards. His last major act was to persuade his compatriots and their government to accept the harsh conditions of the American Loan. Exhausted, Keynes died on Easter Morning, 1946. The *Times*' obituarist made a faultless judgment: a "great" economist; "by his death the country ... lost a very great Englishman" – one who not only did good but who was also truly good himself.

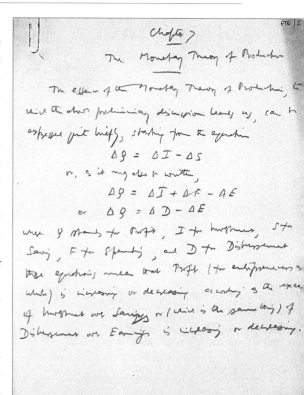

ABOVE The manuscript outline of Maynard Keynes's **The General Theory of Employment, Interest and Money**, published in 1936.

BELOW LEFT John Maynard Keynes (1883-1946) writing his King's Fellowship dissertation. Oil painting of 1908 by Duncan Grant, in King's College, given by Mrs. F.A. Keynes.

BELOW Photograph of Nicky (Lord) Kaldor, by Godfrey Argent, in the Marshall Library of the Faculty of Economics and Politics.

Medicine

Lord Butterfield OBE MD FRCP
Regius Professor Emeritus of Physic; Honorary Fellow of Downing College

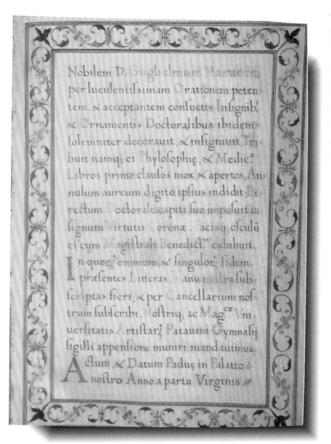

ABOVE John Caius, influential Renaissance man, who studied Medicine in Padua and is said to have been physician to successive Tudor sovereigns. This contemporary portrait hangs in the college he refounded in the name of Gonville and Caius in 1557.

BELOW Diploma of Medicine granted by the University of Padua to William Harvey (who later discovered the circulation of the blood) on 25 April 1602.

Although the University of Cambridge has granted medical degrees since about 1270, the contribution of Cambridge to Medicine should be traced from the establishment in 1540 of the Regius Chair of Physic by Henry VIII. The word Physic in those days meant the study of nature or Natural Philosophy.

RENAISSANCE PHYSIC
At that time, Renaissance scholars were retrieving knowledge from texts of the ancient world. No-one contributed more to this revival of medical learning than John Caius, who went to study in Padua in 1539, returning later to England to practise, to lead the Royal College of Physicians, and to refound a college in his name in Cambridge.

An era of intense experimental and philosophical activity then followed, during which, in the work of William Gilbert and Francis Bacon, there developed the foundations of the experimental method. William Gilbert (?1540-1603), a Fellow of St John's College and relatively unrecognised because his papers were lost in the Great Fire of London, made a major impact in the Europe of the 1560s with his remarkable book *De Magnete*. Galileo, writing in praise of Gilbert, wished he could have made such progress in scientific understanding as had the Colchester-born physician. For many of his investigations into magnetism, Gilbert used spheres of lodestone – magnetic iron ore – corks, iron wires, and basins of water: simple apparatus for exploration of the earth's magnetic field!

The idea that experiments were the means of understanding nature and settling disputed hypotheses led William Harvey (1578-1657) of Caius College to discover and describe the circulation of the blood. Harvey's contribution not only to medical knowledge but also as a radical thinker was quickly appreciated by his contemporaries, and the Royal College of Physicians in London honours him still through its Harveian Oration each October.

THE GROWTH OF MODERN MEDICAL SCIENCE
In subsequent centuries, the concept of Physic contracted to what we now regard as Medicine and Surgery, and Cambridge graduates can be traced making numerous important contributions in these fields. Physiological systems became the subject of specific research, like that of Stephen Hales into blood pressure in the early-eighteenth century. More detailed understanding of bodily functions followed the chemical analyses of body fluids and tissues. The understanding of nutrition expanded rapidly after Frederick Gowland Hopkins was made Professor of Biochemistry in 1914; the portrait showing him working as an experimentalist in his laboratory hangs in the Royal Society, serving to remind us of the growth of knowledge that followed the recognition of body pigments, proteins, and enzymes. The subsequent application of other sciences like X-ray crystallography from Physics, and analysis of amino-acid sequences by computer, led to our grasp of the essentially linear structure of proteins, and so to understanding their synthesis in cells from ribonucleic acid templates derived from the DNA genetic information stored largely in cell nuclei. Leadership in this field, the so-called New Biology, has assured Cambridge of a place in this second revolution in biological thought following Darwinism. Its full impacts remain to be understood.

THE CLINICAL CONTEXT: ADDENBROOKE'S AND THE NHS
To have an effect, Medical Science needs to be conveyed to the sick. Cambridge has maintained pre-eminence in medical teaching within a

Addenbrooke's Hospital on Trumpington Street as it looked in 1834. Lithograph by Day and Haghe from a drawing by W. Fleetwood.

hospital context, and has attracted and stimulated students through the central role of the tutorial system and through the diverse preclinical choice made possible by the Natural Science and Medical Science Triposes, the longstanding examinations for the MD and MChir degrees, and more recently by the new MB/PhD programme. Generations of medical graduates have been encouraged by the teaching of Anatomy (since 1707), Physiology (since the 1870s), Pathology (since 1884), and Biochemistry (since 1914), together with other subjects included in the nineteenth-century attempt to create a full medical course at Old Addenbrooke's Hospital. Sir Edward Paget evolved clinical examinations to test students at the Trumpington Street hospital site: a physician, he was joined in the venture by a surgical dynamo, George Murray Humphrey, who arrived in Cambridge in 1842. Sadly, the early success of this educational experiment produced the cause of its eventual failure: there were too many students for the number of cases in rural Cambridge, especially when compared with the teaching hospitals in overcrowded London.

A much better opportunity for clinical teaching in Cambridge came with the establishment of the East Anglian Region of the National Health Service in 1948. Building on a postgraduate school centred at the University, a whole range of modern health services began to be developed, leading to the opening of the University's Clinical School at New Addenbrooke's Hospital in 1976.

The acquisition of increasingly detailed information about health and disease has widened recognition of the role of environmental and genetic factors. At the same time, the use of increasingly complex diagnostic and therapeutic measures, including transplant surgery, has grown. As a result, the numbers of conditions amenable to treatment and prevention, and the demands for health personnel, for clinics and hospital beds, and for practising doctors, are all increasing. Consequences include more attention to medical ethics, to the reassuring of patients afraid of the workings of the medical establishment, and to the extension of public health measures, such as medical economics and health promotion (limiting, as far as possible, the burden of the NHS on public tax resources).

Experimentation, logical thinking, and the framing of testable hypotheses, in all of which the University has a proud record, will remain essential aspects of future endeavour within the Medical Sciences at Cambridge.

Addenbrooke's was rebuilt in the mid-nineteenth century in response to the new demands of Medical Science both in theory and in practice. This is Griffith Ward in 1896, photographed by Ramsey and Muspratt.

Biological Sciences

Richard D. Keynes CBE ScD FRS
Professor Emeritus of Physiology; Fellow of Churchill College

The term 'Biology' did not come into use until 1813, and the earliest contributions to the Biological Sciences made in Cambridge are considered elsewhere under the mantle of Medicine, the most important being those of William Harvey (1578-1657) and Stephen Hales (1677-1761). Hales made the first direct measurement of blood pressure in horses, but – inspired by the greatest of Cambridge botanists, John Ray (1627-1705) – he also turned his experimental skills to plants, and in his book *Vegetable Staticks* described the rise of sap in vines.

DARWIN AND DARWINISM

After spending two years at Edinburgh University reading Medicine and not liking it, Charles Darwin (1809-1882) was admitted to Christ's College in 1827 as a student of Theology, in which he obtained a degree rather low on the list in 1831. In addition to his sporting activities and beetle collecting, he established close friendships with John Stevens Henslow (1796-1861), Professor of Botany, and with Adam Sedgwick (1785-1873), Professor of Geology, which led to his appointment in 1831 to sail with Captain Robert FitzRoy RN as geologist and naturalist on the voyage of *HMS Beagle* to chart the coasts of the southern part of South America, and afterwards to circumnavigate the globe.

By the time the *Beagle* returned to England in 1836, Darwin had been obliged to abandon a belief in the account of the Creation and the doctrine of the fixity of species current at that time, and was seeking an alternative explanation for his extensive observations on the living and fossil animals and birds of South America. After spending three months in Cambridge, he settled in London and opened a series of notebooks on the *Transmutation of Species*. The principle of natural selection occurred to him after reading Malthus on *Population* in September 1838, but he kept his revolutionary ideas strictly to himself for many years. Soon after his marriage in 1839 to his cousin Emma Wedgwood, he moved to Downe in Kent, where he lived and worked for the rest of his life. His theories remained secret except to his two closest associates Charles Lyell and Joseph Hooker, until in 1858 he received a fateful letter from Alfred Russel Wallace, and after a joint paper with Wallace had been read to the Linnean Society, *On the Origin of Species* at last saw the light of day on 24 November 1859.

Fish preserved in Cambridge from Darwin's **Beagle** voyages.

Although none of Darwin's work was actually carried out in Cambridge, the indoctrination in scientific method that he had received from Henslow, Sedgwick, and others in the University was crucial in determining the direction of his career, as of course was his selection for the voyage of the *Beagle*. One of the measures of his greatness was that he got so much right in revolutionising biological thought without ever knowing about the exact mechanism of inheritance, which had been described in a paper on peas by the Austrian monk Gregor Mendel in 1866, only to lie unnoticed until it was read by William Bateson (1861-1926) in the train from Cambridge to London on 8 May 1900, on his way to lecture to the Royal Horticultural Society. The Cambridge geneticists Bateson, Reginald Punnett (1875-1967), and Ronald Fisher (1890-1962) subsequently did much to establish the basic features of Mendelian genetics and to reconcile them fully with the Darwinian principle of natural selection. The main collection of Darwin's papers is housed in the University Library, where a team of scholars is now engaged on the publication of his entire correspondence; volumes covering the years up to 1860 have appeared, and many more will follow. His spirit lives on in Cambridge, which was a fitting birthplace for the studies of recombinant DNA that are now pervading the whole of Biology.

ABOVE Charles Darwin, 1881: portrait by John Collier.

PHYSIOLOGY AND BIOCHEMISTRY

Other important lines in biological research arose with the establishment of the Physiological Laboratory in 1883, whose first Professor was Michael Foster (1836-1907). Whereas the great pioneers in the subject elsewhere almost invariably began as medical graduates, from Foster's successor J. N. Langley (1852-1925) onwards the Cambridge physiologists were often trained in the Physical Sciences. According to A. V. Hill (1886-1977), who was one of them and shared the 1923 Nobel Prize for his work on muscle, there were probably more great physiologists to the square yard in the old laboratories on the New Museums Site between 1909 and 1914 than in any other place, before or since; and not only because there were so few square yards. They also included the future Nobel Laureates Frederick Gowland Hopkins (1861-1947), founder of Biochemistry and the discoverer of vitamins, and the electrophysiologist E. D. Adrian (1889-1977). The analytical approach to nerve and muscle that had originated with Adrian's teacher Keith Lucas (1879-1916), who was killed in a flying accident while developing instruments at Farnborough during the First World War, later achieved its flowering in Cambridge at the hands of Alan Hodgkin and Andrew Huxley, as was recognised by the award to them of the 1963 Nobel Prize in Physiology and Medicine.

BELOW LEFT Lord Adrian (1889-1977), one of the founders of modern Neurophysiology, who won the Nobel Prize in 1932 for his work on the function of neurons, and went on to become Chancellor of the University of Cambridge.

BELOW The Lucas pendulum, preserved in the Whipple Museum. This device made use of a heavy pendulum to operate knock-down keys in order to generate electric shocks of controllable duration for stimulating muscle and nerve fibres.

Molecular Biology

Ron Laskey MA DPhil FRS
Charles Darwin Professor of Animal Embryology; Fellow of Darwin College

Fred Sanger (1918-), the biochemist whose work in Cambridge on proteins, nucleic acids, and DNA sequencing led him to become the first person ever to receive two Nobel Prizes for Chemistry (in 1958 and 1980).

Molecular Biology is a young subject restricted mostly to the last 50 years. Nevertheless, its impact is enormous and accelerating. It is enabling us to understand how living organisms function and reproduce, and is also allowing new understanding of human diseases and new generations of diagnosis and treatment. The University of Cambridge played crucial roles in the foundation of Molecular Biology, and many of the most important discoveries have been made here, including the discovery of the structure of the hereditary material, DNA, and the first structures of proteins.

THE DNA DOUBLE HELIX AND UNDERSTANDING HEREDITY

One of the most important biological breakthroughs of the century was made in Cambridge in 1953 when James Watson and Francis Crick discovered the double helical structure of DNA. A plaque on the Austin Building on the New Museums Site now marks the location of this crucial discovery. Another former member of Cambridge University, Rosalind Franklin, performed the X-ray diffraction experiments on DNA that led Watson and Crick to propose their model of DNA structure. After Franklin's death, Crick, Watson, and Maurice Wilkins shared the Nobel Prize for Medicine in 1962.

Watson and Crick's model for the structure of DNA triggered immediate advances in our understanding of heredity. It suggested ways in which genetic information could be encoded and it explained how this coded information could be passed from one generation to the next.

PROTEINS: THE MACHINERY OF LIFE

If DNA is the information software of living things, proteins are the hardware. First, they have structural roles, and second, they are catalysts that perform most of the chemical reactions of life. The University of Cambridge has again played a crucial part in our understanding of protein structure and function.

Fred Sanger, working in the Department of Biochemistry, won the first of his two Nobel Prizes for Chemistry in 1958, for determining the specific sequence of the amino-acid building blocks which form the protein insulin. Max Perutz and John Kendrew shared the Nobel Prize for Chemistry in 1962 for solving the three-dimensional structure of proteins, in particular haemoglobin and myoglobin. The influence of Max Perutz on Molecular

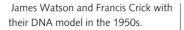

James Watson and Francis Crick with their DNA model in the 1950s.

The Nobel Prize ceremony of 1962. King Gustaf VI Adolf of Sweden presents the Prize for Medicine to Francis Crick, shared with James Watson (standing, centre) and Maurice Wilkins (behind, next to the left). In line to the left of Wilkins stand John Kendrew and (far left) Max Perutz, who shared the Prize for Chemistry.

Biology in Cambridge has been extraordinary. Not only did he found and chair the renowned Medical Research Council Laboratory of Molecular Biology here, but, remarkably, four former members of his own research group shared two Nobel Prizes between them in the same year, 1962 (Crick, Watson, Kendrew, and Perutz).

Other members of Cambridge University working at the MRC Laboratory of Molecular Biology have won three more Nobel Prizes – Aaron Klug (1982) for solving complex three-dimensional structures including viruses and RNA molecules; César Milstein (1984) for discovering a way of producing unlimited supplies of pure, highly specific antibodies (monoclonal antibodies); and Fred Sanger again (1980) for discovering how to determine the information encoded in DNA (DNA sequencing).

GENES AND PROTEINS IN THE PRESENT DECADE

Since the discovery of the DNA double helix, the pace of discovery has accelerated continuously, both in Cambridge and elsewhere. It has resulted in many fundamental discoveries about how living cells and organisms function and develop, but its application is also allowing dramatic advances in diagnosis and treatment of human disease.

Just as antibiotics overcame a generation of infectious diseases, the ability to detect and isolate specific pieces of DNA, i.e. genes, has transformed our knowledge of inherited diseases. For example, genes encoding two inherited predispositions to cancer have recently been identified and isolated in the Department of Pathology. Another collaboration between staff of the Departments of Genetics and Pharmacology is investigating the possibility of correcting the genetic defect in cystic fibrosis by gene therapy.

Proteins too are the subject of major advances at the present time. The ability to manipulate DNA has made it possible to design and produce new proteins. The antibody molecules that defend against infection have already been manipulated successfully in this way in Cambridge.

The techniques of X-ray crystallography and nuclear magnetic resonance are allowing approaches to increasingly challenging problems, such as how proteins interact with each other and how they interact with other molecules like DNA. In this way, work in the University of Cambridge is extending our knowledge from single molecules up to the complex assemblies that form the basis of living organisms. Understanding how these assemblies of molecules function, how they misbehave in diseases such as cancer, and how their behaviour can be regulated provides exciting challenges for the twenty-first century.

BELOW The structure of a protein domain that binds to DNA, determined in the Department of Biochemistry by nuclear magnetic resonance.

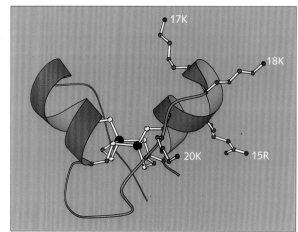

Mathematical Sciences

John Coates PhD FRS
Sadleirian Professor of Pure Mathematics; Fellow of Emmanuel College

ABOVE Isaac Newton (1642-1727): one of the greatest minds Cambridge has produced, and probably the most influential mathematician and physicist of all time. Eighteenth-century terracotta bust by John Michael Rysbrack, in Trinity College.

BELOW Stephen Hawking, current holder of the Lucasian Chair of Mathematics. Drawing by David Hockney.

Known as the Queen of the Sciences, Mathematics is also the indisputable servant of both science and technology. Together with Statistics, it is essential for Medicine and Economics, and indispensable in many other spheres as diverse as industrial processing and the financial sector. The Faculty of Mathematics in the University of Cambridge has been famous for over three centuries. There are no fewer than 24 Mathematical Fellows of the Royal Society now working in Cambridge, three of whom have won the Fields Medal, the mathematical equivalent of the Nobel Prize. The Faculty consists of two Departments, Applied Mathematics and Theoretical Physics, and Pure Mathematics and Mathematical Statistics. In 1992, the University inaugurated the Isaac Newton Institute for Mathematical Sciences, a new international institute for research into Mathematics and its many applications.

Cambridge Mathematics graduates are highly prized and often go on to take up successful careers in a wide variety of fields, from information technology, through operational research and R&D, and general management and management consultancy, to scientific and technological leadership in industry. A very wide range of pure and applied mathematical research is pursued, as are links with industry, but further development is being seriously impaired by a lack of space and facilities. The University needs to build a new centre for the Faculty, on the same site as the Isaac Newton Institute. By combining and developing elements that are at present a mile apart, this will concentrate on one site a strength and quality across the whole spectrum of Mathematical Sciences which is equal to the best in the world.

The Isaac Newton Institute

The Director, Sir Michael Atiyah, President of the Royal Society and Master of Trinity College, said at the Institute's inauguration in 1992: "The idea behind the Institute is to gather some of the best brains in the world to work on extremely difficult problems which will have applications far into the future". Although this is a national institution, its research programmes are strongly international in character. Each programme typically lasts for six months and concentrates on a specialised research theme. The topics cover all branches of the Mathematical Sciences, from Pure Mathematics to Theoretical Physics, Economics, and Mathematical Biology. The early programmes have included Computer Vision, Epidemic Modelling, Geometry and Gravity, and L-Functions and Arithmetic.

Lucasian Professors Past and Present

Cambridge has a number of famous mathematical Chairs. The oldest of these is the Lucasian Professorship, which was founded in 1663. It was first held by Isaac Barrow, who vacated it in 1669 in favour of his student Isaac Newton. In this century, Paul Dirac held it for nearly 40 years, followed by James Lighthill, and since 1979 it has been held by Stephen Hawking. The contributions of these celebrated scientists indicate the variety and importance of Mathematics in Cambridge.

Sir Isaac Newton was probably the greatest mathematician and physicist of all time. The development of calculus by Newton and Leibniz in the seventeenth century allowed mathematicians to understand a vast range of physical problems, including planetary motion. Nowadays, a knowledge of calculus is taken for granted amongst all scientists, economists, and technologists. Among Newton's legacies – which included the study of light, leading to the first reflecting telescope, and his work on gravity – was the foundation of Cambridge's reputation for Mathematics.

Paul Dirac held the Professorship from 1932 to 1969, and was awarded the Nobel Prize for Physics in 1933. He was one of the founding fathers of Quantum Theory, which is basic not only to Physics, but also to Chemistry and Molecular Biology. Dirac's philosophy was that physical laws should have mathematical beauty. He was led by the pursuit of elegant

Mathematics to discover antimatter, of which the positron was the first antiparticle to be discovered. Now, 60 years on, Positron Emission Tomography is an important technique for medical diagnosis. Dirac must be regarded as one of the seminal figures of this century.

James Lighthill came to the Professorship from London University, having previously been director of the Royal Aircraft Establishment at Farnborough. He is best known for his work on aerodynamics, particularly on jet engine noise, the propagation of sonic booms, and supersonic flight, including the design of Concorde. He also made important contributions to the study of the flight of birds and the swimming of fish, and to the understanding, through Mathematics, of the human cardiovascular and auditory systems and of the evolution of dynamically efficient species.

Stephen Hawking has captured popular imagination more than any other scientist since Albert Einstein. His first really important contribution was to show that a consequence of Einstein's theory of General Relativity is that the beginning of the Universe was marked by a fireball known as the 'Big Bang'. His latest findings are that the Universe may after all have no beginning or end. The success of his popular book, *A Brief History of Time*, is testimony to the extent of his appeal to a wider public.

Cosmology

Stephen Hawking CH HonScD PhD FRS
Lucasian Professor of Mathematics; Fellow of Gonville and Caius College

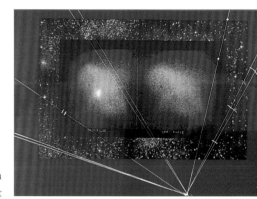

ABOVE Wires, pulses, galaxies: the intermittent signal of a pulsar, with our galaxy behind, and the wires of the Mullard Observatory in the foreground. Graphic by Fran Evelegh.

Cambridge has played a major role in the development of Cosmology in the last 50 years. In 1948 Hermann Bondi, Tommy Gold, and Fred Hoyle, who were all at Cambridge at that time, put forward the Steady State theory of the Universe. As the galaxies moved apart, it was proposed that new galaxies would form from matter that was supposed to be continually in the process of creation. The Universe would have existed forever in more or less the state that we observe today.

The Steady State theory was (in the terminology of Karl Popper) a good scientific theory: it made definite predictions that could be falsified by observations. To test the theory, the Radio Astronomy group at Cambridge under Martin Ryle made surveys of the numbers of radio sources as a function of their strength. They found that there were too many faint sources in relation to strong sources to be compatible with the Steady State theory.

BELOW The telescopes of the University's Mullard Radio Astronomy Observatory, Barton Road, near Cambridge. The Observatory was set up under the influence of Martin Ryle - discoverer of quasars – and his team including Antony Hewish and Jocelyn Bell – who detected the first pulsar. These discoveries altered the course of modern Cosmology.

THE BIG BANG

Ryle's findings ruled out the Steady State and favoured the Big Bang theory, according to which the Universe began with a tremendous explosion about 15 billion years ago. Further theoretical support for the Big Bang came from the singularity theorems proved by Stephen Hawking (at Cambridge) and Roger Penrose (who had been at Cambridge but was by then at Birkbeck College, London). These theorems showed that the Universe and time itself must have had a beginning, if Einstein's theory of General Relativity was correct. At the beginning, Einstein's classical theory would break down, and one would have to pass to a quantum theory of gravity. Such a theory could predict how the Universe began if the Universe obeyed the 'no boundary condition' proposed by James Hartle (of the University of California, Santa Barbara) and Stephen Hawking. This proposal predicts that there should be slight fluctuations in the microwave background radiation – and these have recently been detected by the COBE satellite. Theoretical work at the Cambridge Institute of Astronomy by Martin Rees, Simon White, and others is seeking to show that these small fluctuations led to the formation of galaxies and stars and all the structure we observe in the Universe today.

Physical Sciences

Sir Brian Pippard ScD FRS
Cavendish Professor Emeritus of Physics; Honorary Fellow of Clare Hall and Clare College

Senior staff, c.1980, outside the new Cavendish Laboratory (opened in 1973). The inscription above the doors - **The works of the Lord are great, sought out of all them that have pleasure therein** - is Coverdale's translation of the text in Psalm 111 - **Magna opera Domini exquisita in omnes voluntates ejus** - carved at James Clerk Maxwell's request on the oak doors of the original Cavendish Laboratory in Free School Lane (opened in 1874). The group includes Antony Hewish (fourth from left) and Brian Pippard (third from right).

J. J. Thomson (right) and his most famous pupil, Ernest Rutherford, in Cambridge, c.1933. Thomson is also depicted on p.18.

The Revd John Michell (1724-1793) was a leading figure of British science in the eighteenth century. As a young Fellow of Queens' College he discovered the laws of magnetic attraction, before taking the living of Thornhill where he was equally effective as pastor, geologist, and astronomer. He was the first to note the possibility of Black Holes, and near the end of his life devised, but did not live to perform, a very difficult experiment to measure the gravitational attraction between two masses, which was successfully carried out by Henry Cavendish (1731-1810). Cavendish, after four years as an undergraduate at Peterhouse, did none of his famous work in Cambridge, and would hardly appear in this story but that the Cavendish Laboratory is named after him, at the request of his kinsman the Duke of Devonshire who paid for the original building and its equipment.

EARLY ACHIEVEMENTS AT THE CAVENDISH

The first Cavendish Professor, James Clerk Maxwell, arrived in 1871. He and his successor, Lord Rayleigh, between them occupied the Chair for only 13 years, long enough for their great eminence to make the Laboratory well known, but too short a time to build a characteristic pattern of teaching and research. It was Sir Joseph Thomson – JJ – elected at the age of twenty-seven, who in the 35 years before he became Master of Trinity College created the Cavendish tradition – theory and experiment conceived and brought to fruition with the most economical of means.

Between 1895 when Wilhelm Röntgen discovered X-rays, and 1900 when Max Planck conceived of the quantum of energy, modern Physics was born, and JJ's discovery of the electron in 1897 was central to the revolution in which the Cavendish played a leading role. Owen Richardson's studies of thermionic emission gave secure grounding to the emerging technology of Electronics, while JJ and F. W. Aston showed that light elements as well as the heavy radioactive ones could possess different masses but the same chemical properties. These isotopes provided Aston with his life's work – measuring their masses with such precision that, for example, it became possible to verify that when two nuclei lost energy on combining, they also lost mass in accordance with Einstein's $E=mc^2$. The meteorologist C. T. R. Wilson devised his cloud chamber which fortuitously turned out to be the most valuable instrument available to nuclear physicists for observing the tracks of fast charged particles. All these discoveries contributed to the 17 Nobel Prizes won, so far, for work actually carried out in the Cavendish.

RUTHERFORD AND CHADWICK

The leading nuclear physicist of his day was Lord Rutherford, a New Zealander who had been in 1895 the first research student in the Cavendish from the Dominions. Only three years later he was made a professor, first at McGill before moving to Manchester, and it was in these universities that he carried out the great investigations of radioactivity, the nuclear atom, and the splitting of the nitrogen nucleus that entitle him to a place in the front rank of experimenters. He returned to Cambridge in 1919 to pick up the pieces left by the First World War, and the team he put together – the Nobel Laureates James Chadwick, Patrick Blackett, John Cockcroft, and Ernest Walton, and the many others who made their mark as research students and stayed on, or went off to Chairs all over the world – raised the Cavendish to unrivalled leadership in the world of Physics. Of their many discoveries concerning the constitution of atomic nuclei, none was more important than Chadwick's recognition of the neutron's existence. Its ability to enter nuclei and produce new radioactive isotopes, and to induce fission of uranium, gave birth to the nuclear technology which within a few years was controlling the fate of nations, besides its many other less dramatic applications.

THE BIRTH OF MOLECULAR BIOLOGY

Sir Lawrence Bragg had only just (1912) taken his degree from Trinity College when his insight concerning the reflection of X-rays by crystals started the development of the new discipline of X-ray Crystallography. Those who equated the Cavendish tradition with fundamental (i.e. nuclear) Physics were tempted to doubt if he was a worthy successor to Rutherford. But once the War had ended in 1945 he re-established the research on a broader base, with spectacular success. He encouraged Max Perutz and John Kendrew's heroic success in working out the precise arrangement of the 10,000 or so atoms in a protein molecule, and tolerated the nonconforming Francis Crick and James Watson while they tackled a similar problem with DNA and found the double helix that holds the key to genetic inheritance. These achievements must be accounted as significant as anything done in the Cavendish for their impact on science and in the wider world. In effect Molecular Biology was the creation of a physical laboratory, with a parentage stretching back to young Bragg's inspiration.

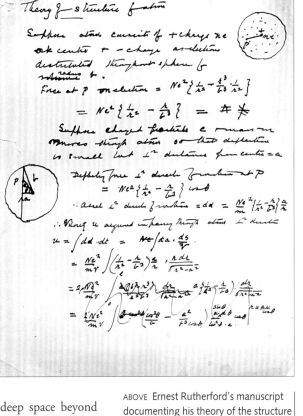

ASTROPHYSICS

Bragg also gave his blessing to the development of Radio Astronomy.

Martin Ryle's synthesis telescopes generated the information about deep space beyond our galaxy which confirmed for most cosmologists the evolutionary nature of the Universe, at that time a highly speculative notion. The remarkable, and rather mysterious, quasars were one of his discoveries, while Antony Hewish and his research student, Jocelyn Bell, detected the first pulsar – the most important single observation, it has been said, in Astrophysics.

ABOVE Ernest Rutherford's manuscript documenting his theory of the structure of the atom.

BELOW Cockcroft and Walton's machine being operated by Ernest Walton, 1932. Their work in Cambridge pioneered the transmutation of atomic nuclei by accelerated particles.

SOLID STATE PHYSICS

After Bragg, Sir Nevill Mott brought a deep theoretical understanding of Solid State Physics, and during his time many fields of more obvious relevance to practical applications came to the fore. This tendency has become even more pronounced since he retired from his Chair (though not from active research). David Shoenberg's experiments provided extraordinarily detailed pictures of how electrons behave in metals. Armed with this knowledge the theorists showed how to explain much that was known only empirically to physicists and metallurgists. Peter Hirsch observed in an electron microscope the motion of dislocations in metals – the process which another Cavendish physicist, G. I. Taylor, had proposed as far back as 1934 to explain why metals were not as strong as they should be. Since Hirsch's observation, electron microscopy as a prime tool in Materials Science has been developed intensively in the Cavendish and elsewhere. And Mott's own interest in disordered semiconductors has inspired wide-ranging experiments of great complexity, and encouraged Physics-based industries increasingly to provide a substantial input of ideas, equipment, and funds, thus keeping the Laboratory in the forefront of research that is at the same time potentially profitable and intellectually rewarding.

Engineering and Chemical Engineering

A. N. Broers PhD ScD FRS FEng
Professor of Electrical Engineering; Master of Churchill College

Jacques Heyman PhD FEng
Emeritus Professor of Engineering; Fellow of Peterhouse

and J. Bridgwater PhD ScD FEng
Professor of Chemical Engineering; Fellow of St Catharine's College

ENGINEERING

Engineers and scientists use the same tools, and because they have a common technical language, there is a tendency to confuse the professions. The distinction, however, is clear: the scientist uses his tools in order to deepen his understanding of the subject, while the engineer uses the same tools to understand how to do something, whether it be to design a turbine blade, an electronic circuit, or a radio telescope – or to drive a tunnel under the Channel.

In the seventeenth century the Royal Society was in no doubt that the 'science' studied by its members should be of immediate and practical use, but the split between 'Engineering' and 'science' was already developing, and as early as 1783 Cambridge University established a Professorship of Experimental Natural Philosophy to ensure that Engineering developed as a discipline in its own right. Of a distinguished succession of holders of the Chair the most significant was Robert Willis; he was elected in 1837, and when he died in 1875 the University realised that an Engineering Department existed in all but name: it was formally established that year.

Since 1875 the Engineering Department has always formed about 10% of the University in terms of numbers of students and staff, and during the Second World War it rose to nearly double that proportion. In 1875 Engineering was a unified discipline, although the subjects taught included mechanisms, structures, strength of materials, prime movers, and steam engines. It is one of the few Schools in the country which retains such a unity, since the Department is not divided into Civil Engineering, Mechanical Engineering, and so on; instead a large graduate staff of about 200 (with 17 professors) covers almost all fields of modern Engineering. Administration is flexible, so that massive resources can be deployed to support developments of the highest class in teaching and research. Examples of notable progress made in the Department since the Second World War include the establishment under the leadership of Sir John Baker of the plastic theory that revolutionised many aspects of structural and mechanical design; the building of the Whittle Laboratory, now a major centre for research in turbomachinery, named after Frank Whittle, designer of the jet engine, who was sent as a mature student to the Department by the RAF; the development by Sir Charles Oatley's group of the ubiquitous scanning electron microscope, thought by many to be the most important scientific instrument developed in the last 50 years, and which was adapted to write the masks for today's electronic chips; and the intense investment in Information Engineering which has led, for example, to a world leadership position in Speech Processing.

In parallel with these research activities, the teaching programme has been completely revised. The undergraduate course for Cambridge engineers now lasts four years, and they graduate not only with the traditional Bachelor of Arts but also with a Master of Engineering. Many students concentrate on Manufacturing Science, and since the first lectures on Management in 1930, Management teaching has been an integral part of the course. Recently the option to study a language has been introduced, to ensure that the Department continues to produce the well-rounded engineer needed for modern industry.

Frank Whittle (1907-), aeronautical engineer who invented the turbojet aircraft engine.

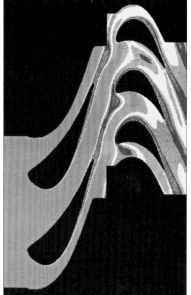

CHEMICAL ENGINEERING

In 1945, the Shell group of companies gave the University a benefaction that led to the foundation of the Department of Chemical Engineering, a department which has throughout its history laid considerable emphasis on its undergraduate teaching. The early course was based on the then unconventional but far-sighted concept that scientific methods could and should be applied to all aspects of the discipline. Graduates of the Department have become leaders within the industry, and several have served as Presidents of the Institution of Chemical Engineers. Members of academic staff are prominent in the industry, one being a member of the Flixborough Enquiry (1974-5). The course now reflects the growth of the importance of safety and the environment.

In research, the Department of Chemical Engineering has played a prominent role in developing the design of chemical reactors and of gas cleaning systems relying on absorption and fluidisation; and is now much concerned with novel processing, energy efficient separation processes, biotechnology, improved catalysts, and modern methods of imaging. Techniques such as the tracking of water motion in a grain, using nuclear magnetic resonance, provide information which raises new scientific issues and new opportunities for effective processing.

ABOVE LEFT Results from the Department of Engineering's Scanning Electron Microprobe group, the largest of its kind in the UK. This technique is unique in giving real-time atomic images, by using a sharp probe to scan over an atomic surface. Here we see the heavily stepped region of the surface of iron silicide.

ABOVE RIGHT Computer simulation of fluid flow around turbine blades.

LEFT Water distribution in a partially cooked grain of wheat after a) 5 minutes, b) 7.5 minutes, c) 10 minutes, and d) 15 minutes. White denotes high water content.

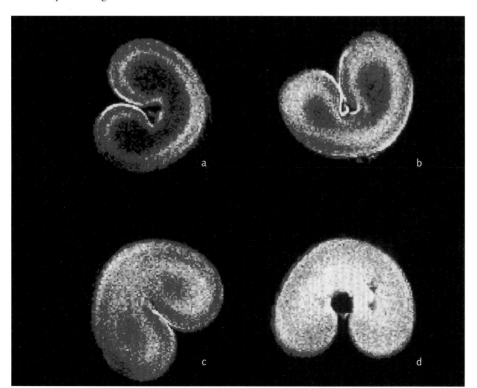

Computer Science and Communications

R. M. Needham FEng FRS
Professor of Computer Systems; Fellow of Wolfson College

BABBAGE AND THE EARLIEST COMPUTER

The idea that machinery could be made to perform repetitive computations is not new: Charles Babbage had his first ideas for a calculating machine before 1820, and pursued them until his death in 1871. His ideas were difficult to implement in a system that was totally mechanical, and progress had to wait until the Harvard Mark 1 machine was constructed in the early-1940s. That machine was basically mechanical but made use of relays and magnetic clutches. It was during the Second World War that ideas for fully electronic calculations emerged, to be exploited once the War had ended.

WILKES AND THE EDSAC

The Computer Laboratory, then called the Mathematical Laboratory, had been founded in 1937 to be a resource for the University on scientific computation. Its development was effectively stopped by the War, but it began to gain momentum in 1946, and under Maurice Wilkes set about building a stored program computer. The 'EDSAC' (Electronic Delay Storage Automatic Computer) worked as a complete system, including input and output peripherals, by May 1949, and was the first such machine anywhere to do so. Wilkes was early to see the need for people who were well trained in the use of computers, and what is now the Diploma in Computer Science began in 1953. Teaching has expanded steadily over the years and there is now a full three-year Tripos in which students learn topics totally unimagined when the Diploma started.

Ever since the early days, the Computer Laboratory has retained its emphasis on the practical side of Computer Engineering – something that distinguishes it from many competing institutions which came into being after you could buy computers and no longer had to make them. Perhaps the most influential contribution to computer architecture was Wilkes' invention of microprogramming, which was for many years a mainstay of system design worldwide.

COMMUNICATIONS AND NETWORKS

In the last 20 years the practical side of the Laboratory's work has been concerned mainly with communication and network systems, where it has been steadily in the front rank of a very competitive field. This continues today, together with a greatly increased presence on the theoretical side of the subject. The Computer Laboratory houses the University Computing Service as well as the academic component, and the Service has made great efforts in support of networking. In 1987 a strategy was proposed under the name of the Project GRANTA which included the idea of the GRANTA Backbone Network, aiming to provide modern high-bandwidth connectivity between all University and college sites. David Hartley succeeded in bringing about an agreement between the University and colleges that resulted in a spasm of digging which left virtually all of the institutions connected by fibre cables running in 25 kilometres of ducts. By 1992 the University had computer network capacity available for almost all of its needs. Furthermore, this effort has positioned the University well to exploit the advantages offered by being an early site for connection to Super JANET, a vastly upgraded national academic network brought to Cambridge in early 1993.

Computer Science and Communications move fast, and nobody knows where the action will be in five years' time. This is both stimulating and challenging. It is not easy both to remain influential in research and to continue to produce well-informed, independent, 'can-do' young people; but this is what the Computer Laboratory proposes to stay good at.

TOP Charles Babbage (1792-1871). Portrait by Samuel Lawrence, 1845, in the National Portrait Gallery.

ABOVE A fragment of Babbage's early-nineteenth-century 'Difference Engine', a calculating machine which he never completed but which heralded later inventions leading to the modern computer.

BELOW A spray of optic fibres conducting red light. Cambridge is in the forefront of computer networking making use of the latest optic-fibre technology.

List of Exhibits

The list should be used in conjunction with the information leaflet available at the exhibition. Numbers correspond to object numbers in cases. These are subject to alteration.

Entrance to the exhibition
University chest, iron with multiple locks, 15th cent. [OS]

1 Founders & Foundations

This section of the exhibition contains manuscripts and other material relating to the early history of the University, including one of the University's great treasures, the *Canterbury Gospels*. A series of maps illustrates the expansion of both University and town.

1 *Old Proctor's Book*, c.1390 with later insertions [UL]
2 *Junior Proctor's Book*, c.1398 -1784 [UL]
3 Indenture, for a perpetual commemoration of Henry VII, 1504 [UL]
4 University Statutes granted by Elizabeth I, 1570 [UL]
5 Grant of arms to the University, 1573 [UL]
6 Grant of arms to Regius Professors, 1590 [UL]
7 *Liber Privilegorium*, 1587 [UL]
8 '*Matthew Stokys's Book*', c.1578 [UL]
9 Emmanuel College charter, with Hilliard portrait of Elizabeth I, 1584 [EM]
10 *The Canterbury Gospels*, Italian, vellum, 6th cent. [CC]
11 *Henry VIII*, after Holbein, oil on canvas, mid 16th cent. [OS]
12 *Commemoration of Benefactors*, 1639/1640 [UL]
13 *Commemoration of Benefactors*, 1842 [UL]
14 Votes cast for J. Dupont as Vice-Chancellor, 1669 [UL]
15 Selection of paper votes for University officers, 1612-1700 [UL]
16 Braun and Hogenberg, Map of Cambridge, 1575, from *Civitates Orbis Terrarum* [UL]
17 David Loggan, Map of Cambridge, originally published in *Cantabrigia illustrata*, 1688 [UL]
18 W. Custance, *A new plan of the University and Town*, 1798 [UL]
19 R. G. Baker, *Baker's new map of the University & Town*, 1830 [UL]
20 Cromwell's death mask, painted plaster cast [SID]
21 Menu, for the Vice-Chancellor's dinner on the installation of Prince Albert as Chancellor, St Catharine's College, 5 July 1847 [UL]
22 Menu, for similar dinner at Trinity College, 6 July 1847 [UL]

23 Subscription Book, with signatures of Eisenhower and Montgomery upon proceeding to Honorary Degrees, 11 Oct. 1946 [UL]
24 *Esquire Bedell's mace*, silver, c.1626 [FM, on loan from the University of Cambridge]
25 Cobbould, *The administration of weights and measures in Tudor Cambridge*, oil on canvas, 18th cent. [OS]
26 - 37 Weights and measures, mainly bronze, made and assayed in London, 1574 onwards [CR]
38 Barley measure, cast iron, 1641 [OS]
39 Painted hatchment with arms of Charles II, c.1650 [CR]
40 Robert Peake, *Charles I while Duke of York*, oil on canvas, painted to commemorate his visit to the University, 1613 [OS]

The Hamilton Kerr Institute, founded in 1978 as a sub-department of the Fitzwilliam Museum, to train conservators of paintings and drawings, has cleaned and conserved the above painting (40). Photographs of the conservation work, showing X-ray details of another painting beneath the surface, are on display.

2 Women at Cambridge

A number of women, particularly the Countess of Pembroke, Lady Margaret Beaufort, and the Countess of Sussex, were instrumental in the foundation of some of the earliest Cambridge colleges. The first women's colleges were Newnham, founded in 1871, and Girton, which moved to Cambridge in 1873 after opening in Hitchin, Hertfordshire, in 1869. However, it was not until 1948 that women were admitted as full members of the University. Copies of archive photographs from Girton and Newnham Colleges are displayed in this section, with original material from both colleges.

1 Atelier of Jean Pucelle, *Breviary* of Marie de St Pol, Countess of Pembroke, before 1377 [UL]
2 J. Faber, *Lady Margaret Beaufort*, mezzotint, 1714 [OS]
3 Rudolph Lehmann, *Emily Davies*, oil on canvas, 1880 [G]
4 List of benefactors to proposed new college, 1869 [G]
5 College prospectus, 1869 [G]
6 Photograph of Girton College fire brigade, 1898 [G]

7 Girton fire brigade brass inkwell, late 19th cent. [G]
8 Girton fire brigade wooden rattle, 1901 [G]
9 George du Maurier, *'Honour to Agnata Frances Ramsay!'*, cartoon for *Punch*, 1887 [G]
10 *Alice Gruner's Room, North Hall*, Newnham, watercolour, 1886 [N]
11 Photograph of Miss Katherine Jex-Blake, Mistress of Girton, 1916 [G]
12 Degree certificate issued to Miss Jex-Blake, 1882 [G]
13 Degree issued to Miss Jex-Blake, 1948 [G]
14 Banner, designed by Mary Lowndes, worked by students of Girton and Newnham Colleges, 1908 [N]
15 Henry Lamb, *Jane Pernel Strachey*, oil on canvas, 1926 [N]
16 Subscription book opened to show the signature of Queen Elizabeth (now the Queen Mother) upon proceeding to an Honorary Degree, 1948 [UL]

3 University Collections

The West Room is hung with paintings from the Fitzwilliam Museum. At one end of the room is a display of college plate, including the *Essex Cup* given to the University by Chancellor Robert

Key	
AA	Museum of Archaeology and Anthropology
BFBS	British & Foreign Bible Society
CAI	Gonville & Caius College
CavL	Cavendish Laboratory
CC	Corpus Christi College
CCL	Cambridge Central Library
CL	Computer Laboratory
CR	Combination Room
CUBC	Cambridge University Boat Club
CUP	Cambridge University Press
DOW	Downing College
EM	Emmanuel College
FM	Fitzwilliam Museum
G	Girton College
JE	Jesus College
JN	St John's College
K	King's College
M	Magdalene College
MRC	MRC Laboratory of Molecular Biology
N	Newnham College
OS	Old Schools
PEM	Pembroke College
SM	Sedgwick Museum
SID	Sidney Sussex College
T	Trinity College
UL	University Library
W	Whipple Museum
ZM	Zoology Museum
and other individual lenders as indicated	

Devereux in 1598, and mounted silver from the Fitzwilliam. There are separate displays from Kettle's Yard, the Museum of Archaeology & Anthropology, and a case of Korean porcelain from the Fitzwilliam Museum.

Fitzwilliam Museum paintings
(all oil on canvas)

1 N. V. Diaz de la Pena (1807-1876) *Landscape*, c. 1870
2 M. Hobbema (1638-1709) *Wooded landscape with cottages*, 1665
3 G. von Honthorst (1590-1656) *William, Earl of Craven*, 1642
4 G. B. Gaulli, Il Baccicio (1639-1709) *The 3 Maries at the empty sepulchre*, c. 1684
5 H. Goltzius (1558-1617) *Vertumnus & Pomona*,1615
6 Carlo Dolci (1616-1686) *Sir Thomas Baines*, c.1665-70
7 Carlo Dolci (1616-1686) *Sir John Finch*, c.1665-70
8 - 19 Jacob van Huysum (c.1687-1740) *Twelve months of the year. January* to *December* (series of 12 paintings), 1732-4

Buffet of college plate, with additional mounted silver from the Fitzwilliam Museum

1 *Essex cup*, silver-gilt, 1592/3 [FM on loan from the University of Cambridge]
2 *Swan mazer*, maple wood with silver-gilt mounts, late 14th cent.   [CC]
3 *Anathema cup*, silver-gilt, 1481/2 [PEM]
4 *Foundress' cup*, silver-gilt, mid 15th cent.   [PEM]
5 *Founder's cup and cover*, silver-gilt, Antwerp, 1541/2   [EM]
6 *Falcon cup*, silver-gilt, Antwerp, 1561   [Clare]
7 *Founder's cup*, silver-gilt with enamel detail, France, c.1300   [TH]
8 *Matthew Parker's chalice and cover*, silver-gilt, 1569/70   [CAI]
9 *Matthew Parker's flagon*, silver-gilt, 1570/1   [CAI]
10 Isnik jug, stoneware with silver-gilt mounts, c.1560   [FM]
11 'Tigerware' jug, English earthenware, 1558/9   [FM]
12 Bowl, Chinese porcelain with silver-gilt mounts, c.1580   [FM]
13 Cup and cover, trochus shell, 17th cent.   [FM]
14 Cup and cover, coconut, 16th/17th cent.   [FM]
15 Cup and cover, coconut, 16th/17th cent.   [FM]

16 Reliquary, German, crystal with silver-gilt mounts, 16th cent.   [FM]
17 Ostrich egg cup, silver mount, 1805/6   [FM]
18 Cup and cover, lapis lazuli with silver-gilt mount, 1826/7   [FM]
19 'Askos' water jug, glass with silver mount, 1839/40   [FM]
20 Decanter designed by William Burges, glass set with stones, gems, silver, 1865/6   [FM]
21 Flagon designed by William Butterfield, glass with silver mount, 1865/6   [FM]
22 Doulton jug, stoneware with silver mount, 1874   [FM]

Korean porcelain from the Fitzwilliam Museum

1 Melon-shaped ewer and cover with basin, Celadon ware, Koyro dynasty
2 Small ewer, Celadon ware, Koyro dynasty
3 Ewer and cover, Celadon ware, Koyro dynasty
4 Black ewer, Koyro dynasty
5 Bottle with floral decoration, Celadon ware, Koyro dynasty
6 Ovoid jar, white porcelain, Choson dynasty
7 Ovoid jar with crane and tortoise, blue and white porcelain, Choson dynasty

University Museum of Archaeology & Anthropology
(Nos 1 - 3 were collected by Captain Cook, no. 5 by A. Maudslay, no. 6 by Baron von Hügel, no. 7 by E. Evans-Pritchard, no. 8 by G. Bateson)

1 Maori paddle club, wood, haliotis shell, late 18th cent.
2 Bone figure, Canadian N.W. coast, bone and animal skin, late 18th cent.
3 Anthropomorphic food bowl, Hawaii, wood, shell, late 18th cent.
4 'Buk' mask, Torres Strait, wood, late 19th cent.
5 'Spiriti' club, Fiji, wood, c.1875
6 'Root' club, Fiji, wood with whale ivory inlay, c.1875
7 'Kambu Buda' pot, Zande, earthenware, c.1920s
8 Mask, Iatmul, wood, shells, boar tusk, c.1920s

Kettle's Yard
The display shows a group of paintings, furniture, and ceramics displayed together to recreate the atmosphere of this house, given to the University by Jim Ede in 1966.

1 Ben Nicholson, *Abstract*, gouache on board, 1941
2 Alfred Wallis, *French lugsail fishing boat*, oil on card
3 Alfred Wallis, *Houses*, oil on card
4 Joan Miro, *Tic Tic*, oil on canvas, 1927
5 H. Gaudier Brzeska, *Female torso*, marble grains in resin, cast in 1975 from the 1913 original in the Tate Gallery
6 Lucie Rie, bowl, 1974
7 Side table, English, oak, 18th cent.
8 Pair of glass decanters, English, 1820/25 (belonged to George Moore)
9 Cider press screw, French, 18th/19th cent.
10 Ben Nicholson, *Kings and Queens*, linocut on cloth
11 Corner cabinet, French, mahogany, 18th cent., dislayed with English and French porcelain, and Bohemian glass, mainly 19th cent.

4 Cambridge Architecture

University and college architecture is shown in the exhibition through a display of architectural drawings and models, a continuous videodisc programme with 130 images of Cambridge colleges (lent by the Wellcome Trust), and a slide sequence showing examples of 20th-cent. University architecture.

1 N. Hawksmoor, *King's College Chapel, East End*, pencil drawing, c.1712   [K]
2 Cambridge University Almanack, *King's West Front*, engraving, 1802   [UL]
3 Cambridge University Almanack, *Jesus College*, engraving, 1805   [UL]
4 Cambridge University Almanack, *Sidney Sussex College*, engraving, 1809   [UL]
5 Cambridge University Almanack, *Downing College*, engraving, 1812   [UL]
6 W. Wilkins, *Proposed ground plan of Downing*, ink and watercolour, 1822   [DOW]
7 W. Wilkins, *Elevation of South Block, Downing*, ink and watercolour, post-1812   [DOW]
8 J. Wyattville, *Garden Front, Sidney Sussex*, watercolour, c.1823   [SID]
9 C. R. Cockerell, *Building work in progress on the Science Museum and Library*, watercolour, 1837-40   [OS]
10 W. Waterhouse, *Girton College*, watercolour, 1887   [G]
11 B. Champneys, design for Newnham Hall, *Building News*, 1874   [N]

12 B. Champneys, design for North Hall, Newnham, *Building News*, 1881 [N]

13 F. Terry, *Construction of the Maitland Robinson Library, Downing*, ink drawing of the library by Quinlan Terry, 1992 [DOW]

14 Model of Wren Chapel, Pembroke c.1665 [PEM]

15 Norman Foster, model and colour photos of Sidgwick Site, 1990 [Sir Norman Foster and Partners]

16 Michael Hopkins, model of new theatre at Emmanuel, 1993 [EM]

5 Philosophy

This section of the exhibition examines the work of three of Cambridge's most influential philosophers, **Bertrand RUSSELL** (1872-1970), **G. E. MOORE** (1873-1958) and **Ludwig WITTGENSTEIN** (1889-1951). Contemporary Cambridge philosophy is represented by material from the forthcoming multi-volume *Encyclopedia of Philosophy*, edited and with many contributions from within the University's Department of Philosophy.

1 John Wheatley, *Portrait of Bertrand Russell*, pencil on paper, 1947 [T]

2 B. Russell, *Principia Mathematica*, 3 vols. 1910-13 [UL]

3 B. Russell, *An Enquiry into Meaning and Truth*, 1940 [UL]

4 B. Russell, letter to Moore, about Wittgenstein's recent work, May 1930 [UL]

5 Eliot & Fry, photograph of George Moore, c.1935 [UL]

6 G. E. Moore, *Principia Ethica*, copy belonging to J. M. Keynes, with his annotations, 1903 [K]

7 G. E. Moore, autograph ms. *Proof of an External World*, Nov.1939 [UL]

8 L. Wittgenstein, letter to Moore requesting his presence at a talk at the Moral Sciences Club, Nov. 1946 [UL]

9 L. Wittgenstein, copy of letter sent to B. Russell from his prisoner-of-war camp, 1919. Russell forwarded the letter to Moore [UL]

10 L. Wittgenstein, *Tractatus Logico-philosophicus*, 1921 [UL]

11 L. Wittgenstein, notebook (111), July-Sept. 1931 [T]

12 L. Wittgenstein, notebook (136), Dec. 1947-Jan.1948 [T]

13 L. Wittgenstein, *Philosophische Untersuchungen*, 1953 [UL]

14 L. Wittgenstein, 8 postcards and a Christmas card sent to Gilbert Pattison, 1930s [T]

6 Engineering, Computing, Technology

This display is based around the Whipple Museum's fragment of the Difference Engine, a calculating machine built by **Charles BABBAGE** (1792-1871), Professor of Mathematics and pioneer computer scientist. The display demonstrates the progression from manual and mechanical calculating machines through to modern computers. Current work in the field is represented by the Autostereo display, a joint project between the Department of Engineering and the Computer Laboratory.

1 Slide rule, designed by William Oughtred, made by Elias Allen, brass, c.1630 [W]

2 Set of drawing instruments, made by John Rowley, brass, steel, wood, case covered with fish-skin, 1703 [W on loan from T]

3 Sector, made by John England, brass, 1703 [W on loan from T]

4 Set of 'Napier's Bones', brass, wood, in boxwood box, 1720 [W on loan from FM]

5 Fragment of Babbage's Difference Engine, brass, steel, paper, wooden base (demonstration model assembled by Babbage's son Henry, after his father's death) [W]

6 'Millionaire' calculating machine, made by Hans Egli, Zurich, patented by O. Steiger, 1895 [CL]

7 Autostereo display, 1994 [CL]

7 Physical Sciences

With 17 Nobel Prize winners to its credit, the Old Cavendish Laboratory in Free School Lane is renowned as the birthplace of modern Physics and Molecular Biology. This display looks at the work of two Nobel Prize winners, both Directors of the Cavendish Laboratory: **J. J. THOMSON** (1856-1940), Professor of Experimental Physics, who discovered the electron, and his pupil **Ernest RUTHERFORD** (1871-1937), a pioneer in subatomic Physics. The Cavendish Laboratory and the Department of Physics have now moved to West Cambridge; the exhibition includes photographs of a number of current research projects, including the single electron memory.

1 Arthur Hacker RA, *J. J. Thomson*, oil on canvas, 1903 [CavL]

2 J. J. Thomson, *Recollections and Reflections*, 1936 [UL]

3 J. J. Thomson, X-ray tube, made by Everett, glass and steel, 1896 [CavL]

4 J. J. Thomson, discharge tube (replica), glass and steel [CavL]

5 Palmer Clarke, *Photograph of Lord Rutherford*, 1930s [CCL]

6 E. Rutherford, scientific notebook containing his notes *Theory of structure of atom*, 1912 [UL/CavL]

7 E. Rutherford, nuclear disintegration chamber, wood, metal, glass, c.1919 (replica) [CavL]

8 E. Rutherford, *Radioactive substances and their radiations*, 1913 (Rutherford's initialled copy) [Dr Dean]

9 Photograph of Wilson's cloud chamber, 1912 [Dr Dean]

10 Photograph of alpha tracks from thorium, 1922 [Dr Dean]

11 Photograph of alpha tracks from actinium, 1927 [Dr Dean]

12 Pedestal desk used by Cavendish Directors including Maxwell, Rayleigh, Thomson, and Rutherford; English, 1830s [CavL]

A number of copies of archive photographs from the Cavendish Laboratory are also displayed.

8 Economics & Business

The Economics display concentrates on the work of **J. Maynard KEYNES** (1883-1946), Current research in

Key	
AA	Museum of Archaeology and Anthropology
BFBS	British & Foreign Bible Society
CAI	Gonville & Caius College
CavL	Cavendish Laboratory
CC	Corpus Christi College
CCL	Cambridge Central Library
CL	Computer Laboratory
CR	Combination Room
CUBC	Cambridge University Boat Club
CUP	Cambridge University Press
DOW	Downing College
EM	Emmanuel College
FM	Fitzwilliam Museum
G	Girton College
JE	Jesus College
JN	St John's College
K	King's College
M	Magdalene College
MRC	MRC Laboratory of Molecular Biology
N	Newnham College
OS	Old Schools
PEM	Pembroke College
SM	Sedgwick Museum
SID	Sidney Sussex College
T	Trinity College
UL	University Library
W	Whipple Museum
ZM	Zoology Museum
and other individual lenders as indicated	

Management Studies is represented by projects of international interest undertaken by members of the *Judge Institute*, established in 1990.

1. Duncan Grant, *Portrait of J. M. Keynes*, oil on canvas, 1908 [K]
2. Vanessa Bell, *The Keynes-Keynes*, portrait of Keynes and his wife Lydia Lopokova, oil, gouache, and charcoal on paper laid on board, c.1927 [K]
3. Lloyd George, *We can conquer unemployment*, 1929 [K]
4. J. M. Keynes, *Can Lloyd George do it?* 1929 [K]
5. J. M. Keynes, ms outline of *The General Theory of Employment, Interest and Money*, c.1936 [K]
6. J. M. Keynes, *The General Theory of Employment, Interest and Money*, 1936 [K]
7. J. M. Keynes, text of speech, 3 July 1944 [K]
8. R. C. Leffingwell, letter with poem on Bretton Woods, 8 July 1944 [K]
9. *Fortune* magazine, with cartoon of Keynes by David Low, 1945 [K]
10. Ariosto, *Orlando Furioso*, Keynes' copy, inscribed by Jane Austen and Virginia Woolf, 1783 [K]

9 Mathematics & Cosmology

Cambridge Mathematics is represented by displays on two Lucasian Professors of Mathematics, **Sir Isaac NEWTON** (1642-1727) and the current Professor, **Stephen HAWKING**. An interactive video programme presents recent research and modern applications of Newton's theories by the Department of Applied Math-ematics and Theoretical Physics, the Department of Pure Mathematics and Mathematical Statistics, and the Isaac Newton Institute for Mathematical Sciences.

1. J. Vanderbank, *Portrait of Sir Isaac Newton*, oil on canvas, 1725 [T]
2. F. Roubilliac (attrib.), death mask of Newton, plaster, 1727 [T]
3. I. Newton, undergraduate expenses notebook, 1661 [T]
4. I. Newton, framed lock of hair [T]
5. Walking stick, said to have belonged to Newton, late 17th cent. [T]
6. I. Newton, *Philosophiae naturalis principia mathematica*, annotated by the author, 1687 [T]
7. I. Newton, letter to Hooke on gravity, 1679 [T]
8. I. Newton, *Opticks*, with ms alterations by the author, 1704 [UL]
9. Prism, which may have belonged to Newton, late 17th cent. [W on loan from T]

10. Trade card of John Yarwell, 1683, showing similar prism, with notes verso by Newton [W]
11. Receipt by Christopher Cocke for a 14-foot telescope and a 5-glass microscope, 1668/9 [UL]
12. G. B. Pittoni, with D. and G. Valeriani, *Allegorical monument to Sir Isaac Newton*, oil on canvas, c.1725 [FM]
13. Table orrery, George Adams, c.1790 [WM]
14. D. Hockney, *Portrait of Stephen Hawking*, pencil drawing, 1978 [CAI]

10 Medicine

William HARVEY (1578-1657), the physician who determined the circulation of the blood, is the central figure in this section of the exhibition. There is an additional display on the work of *Sir F. Gowland Hopkins* (1861-1947) who won the Nobel Prize for Physiology & Medicine in 1929, for his discovery of vitamins. Contemporary developments are illustrated by research projects at the Clinical School, into brain repair, diabetes, multiple sclerosis and, transplantation.

1. W. Harvey, facsimile of Diploma of Doctor of Medicine, granted by the University of Padua; Chiswick Press, 1908 [UL]
2. W. Harvey, *Prelectiones anatomiae universalis*, reprint, 1886 [UL]
3. W. Harvey, *De motu cordis*, 1628 [M]
4. W. Harvey, *Exercitatio anatomica de circulatione sanguinis*, 1649 [UL]
5. W. Harvey, *De generatione animalium* with ms poem to Harvey, 1651 [UL]
6. Petrified skull in Elizabethan wooden box [SID]
7. W. Harvey, letter to Dr Ward about showing the skull to Charles I [SID]
8. Caduceus, silver with enamel, originally belonging to Dr John Caius, pioneer of dissection, mid-16th cent. [CAI]
9. College seal of Dr Caius, silver, 1557 [CAI]
10. Anatomical boxwood figure and ivory skeleton in box, presented to the University in 1591 by John Banster [UL]
11. Stephen Hales, *Haemastaticks*, 1733 [CC]
12. J. G. Hopkins, *Tryptophan Metabolism* notebook, 1912 [UL]
13. Poster advertising an Anglo-Batavian lecture by Hopkins, 1924 [UL]
14. Nobel Prize telegram, to Prof. Sir F. Gowland Hopkins, 1929 [UL]

15. Cartoon from *Dagens Nyheter*, showing Hopkins and his wife, 1929 [UL]

11 Biological Sciences

The voyage of **Charles DARWIN** (1809-1882) on HMS Beagle from 1831-6 forms the centrepiece of this section of the exhibition, with a range of specimens on display. Also on show is the manuscript of Darwin's major work, *The Origin of Species by Means of Natural Selection*, 1859. Current research is shown through photographs of projects in the Department of Zoology, including the work of behavioural ecologists.

1. Sir W. B. Richmond, *Portrait of Charles Darwin*, oil on canvas, 1879/80 [Dept. of Zoology]
2. Albert Way, *'Go it Charlie!'* and *'Darwin and his HOBBY'*, drawing showing Darwin riding a beetle, c.1828 [UL]
3. Box of insect specimens collected by Darwin as an undergraduate [ZM]
4. Charles Darwin, list of his father's objections to his going on the Beagle voyage, 1831 [UL]
5. Charles Darwin, list of specimens brought back on HMS Beagle, c.1836 [UL]
6. Conrad Martens, *Slinging the Monkey at Port Desire*, watercolour in an album made on the Beagle, 25 Dec. 1833 [UL]

Nos 7 - 11 were collected by Darwin on the Beagle voyage:

7. Two jars of fish [ZM]
8. Loggerhead goose, collected in the Falkland Islands [ZM]
9. Sample of grossular prehnite rock, collected from Wollaston Island, Tierra del Fuego, Chile [SM]
10. Samples of quartzite, collected from the Blue Mountains, New South Wales [SM]
11. Sample of 'Cat's Eye', collected from the Cape of Good Hope, S. Africa [SM]

12. Darwin's compound microscope, made by James Smith, c.1846 [W]
13. Charles Darwin, first outline of species theory, 1842 [UL]
14. Charles Darwin, page from original manuscript of *On the Origin of Species*, c.1859 [UL]
15. Charles Darwin, *The Origin of Species by Means of Natural Selection*, 1st ed. with author's annotations, 1859 [UL]
16. Printed invitation to Darwin's funeral at Westminster Abbey, 1882 [ZM]
17. Dodo skeleton (composite), the bones collected on Mascarene Island, near Mauritius, 1866 [ZM]

12 Molecular Biology

The discovery in 1953 of the structure of DNA by **Francis CRICK** (1916-) and **James WATSON** (1928-), incorporating the research of Rosalind Franklin (1921-1958), is one of the 20th cent.'s most famous achievements. Other Nobel Prize winning biologists followed this success, including Frederick Sanger, a double Nobel laureate, for work on amino and nucleic acids; Max Perutz, for research into the structure of haemoglobin; and John Kendrew, for work on myoglobin. A photographic display shows some of the modern applications of DNA research, including genetic medicine and protein engineering.

1. F. Crick & J. Watson, 'Molecular Structure of Nucleic Acids', *Nature*, vol. 171, 1953 [UL]
2. Revolving model of DNA, brass, steel, plastic, c.1962 [MRC]
3. W. L. Bragg, *Max Perutz*, pencil drawing, 1964 [MRC]
4. W. L. Bragg, *John Kendrew*, crayon drawing, 1964 [MRC]
5. Model of the structure of myoglobin, expanded styrofoam on metal former, Kendrew, 1957 [MRC]
6. Electron density map of ß-chain human deoxyhaemoglobin, perspex, Perutz, c.1967 [MRC]
7. X-ray precession camera with crystal and laser, c.1970 [MRC]
8. Free-standing model of tobacco mosaic virus, A. Klug, expanded polystyrene and polythene, 1958 [MRC]

13 Literature

This section of the exhibition concentrates on **Alfred, Lord TENNYSON** (1809-1892), whose major poetic achievement, *In Memoriam A.H.H.*, was an elegy on the death of his undergraduate companion at Trinity, Arthur Hallam. Contem-porary literature is represented by manuscripts from four of the University's many poets and authors, with photo-graphs of other Cambridge literary figures, past and present.

1. T. Woolner, *Alfred, Lord Tennyson*, marble bust, 1857 [T]
2. G. F. Watts, *Portrait of Tennyson*, oil on canvas, 1890 [T]
3. J. Harden, *Tennyson and friends on a steamer*, watercolour, 1830 [T]
4. Tennyson, *In Memoriam A.H.H.*, manuscript, 1834-42 [T]
5. Tennyson, *The Lady of Shalott*, manuscript, 1830s [T]
6. *The Poems of Tennyson*, ed. C. Ricks, pub. Longman, 1987 [T]

7 - 9. Manuscripts lent by the authors Peter Ackroyd, A. S. Byatt (*Possession*), Ted Hughes
10. Transcript of radio adaptation of his book *Hitchhiker's Guide to the Galaxy*, written and lent by Douglas Adams

14 Classics & Archaeology

The textual critic **Richard BENTLEY** (1662-1742) and the pioneering archaeologist **Dorothy GARROD** (1892-1968) are the main figures in this display, although there is also a portrait of Jane Harrison, the classicist and social anthropologist. *The McDonald Institute for Archaeological Research* is shown, with information about recent research into the ancestry of modern wheat, using molecular genetics.

1. After Thornhill, *Portrait of Bentley*, oil on canvas, c.1710 [JN]
2. R. Bentley, letter with marriage proposal, 1700 [T]
3. *Q. Horatius Flaccus*, edited by Bentley, 1711 (Newton's copy) [T]
4. J. Milton, *The Poetical Works of Mr John Milton*, vol 1, annotated by Bentley, 1720 [UL]
5. J. Milton, *Paradise Lost*, edited by Bentley, 1732 [UL]
6. H. Lamb, *Portrait of Dorothy Garrod*, black chalk, 1949 [N]
7. Group of tools excavated by Prof. Garrod at Mount Carmel, Palestine, Paleolithic period [AA]
8. Romano-British slab from near Hadrian's Wall, carved stone (described in Camden's *Britannia*) [AA]
9. Augustus John, *Portrait of Jane Ellen Harrison*, oil on canvas, 1909 [N]

15 Cambridge & Humanism

This display concentrates on **Desiderius ERASMUS** (1466-1536), who taught at Cambridge for three years, and **Thomas CRANMER** (1489-1556), Cambridge don and later martyred Archbishop of Canterbury, who was largely responsible for *The Book of Common Prayer*. The display also looks at the English Bible in the 16th cent.. Current projects in the Divinity School are shown, including the Starbridge lectureship, and the creation of the Centre for Advanced Religious and Theological Studies (CARTS).

1. *Portrait of Thomas Cranmer*, oil on panel, 16th cent. [JE]
2. D. Erasmus, *Testamentum Novum Graece*, pub. J. Froben, Basle, 1527 (copy from Cranmer's library) [JE]

3. D. Erasmus, *Testamentum Novum*, 1535 (from Cranmer's library) [UL]
4. Jacques Lefevre d'Etaples, *Commentarii initiatorii in quatuor evangelia*, 1522 (from Cranmer's library) [UL]
5. D. Erasmus, *An Exhortation to the Diligent Studye of Scripture*, 1529 [UL]
6. Thomas More, *The Confutation of Tyndale's Answers*, 1532 (from Cranmer's library) [JE]
7. Coverdale, *Biblia*, 1535, title page by Hans Holbein the younger [BFBS/UL]
8. *The Byble in Englyshe*, 1540, preface by Thomas Cranmer [UL]
9. *The Book of Common Prayer*, 1552 [UL]
10. John Legate, *The Bible*, 1591 (first English Bible printed by CUP) [BFBS/UL]
11. T. and J. Buck, *The Bible*, 1629 (first CUP printing of the 1611 Authorized Version) [UL]
12. Oak bench, formerly in University chapel, 16th cent. [UL]

16 History

The works of **Lord MACAULAY** (1800-1860) and of the legal historian **F. W. MAITLAND** (1850-1906) form the centrepiece of the History section of the exhibition, with additional displays of Lord Acton's *Cambridge Modern History*, and the remarkable 8th-cent. manuscript of Bede's *Ecclesiastical History of the*

Key

AA	Museum of Archaeology and Anthropology
BFBS	British & Foreign Bible Society
CAI	Gonville & Caius College
CavL	Cavendish Laboratory
CC	Corpus Christi College
CCL	Cambridge Central Library
CL	Computer Laboratory
CR	Combination Room
CUBC	Cambridge University Boat Club
CUP	Cambridge University Press
DOW	Downing College
EM	Emmanuel College
FM	Fitzwilliam Museum
G	Girton College
JE	Jesus College
JN	St John's College
K	King's College
M	Magdalene College
MRC	MRC Laboratory of Molecular Biology
N	Newnham College
OS	Old Schools
PEM	Pembroke College
SM	Sedgwick Museum
SID	Sidney Sussex College
T	Trinity College
UL	University Library
W	Whipple Museum
ZM	Zoology Museum
and other individual lenders as indicated	

English People. Current work in the History Faculty is shown by posters for the four M. Phil. degrees, and page proofs from the 1st volume of the forthcoming *Cambridge Medieval History*, edited within the Faculty and published by the University Press.

1 Sir Francis Grant, *Portrait of Lord Macaulay*, oil on canvas, 1853   [T]
2 Undergraduate letter from Macaulay to his father, 1818   [T]
3 T. B. Macaulay *Journal*, 1838-49   [T]
4 Photographs of Macaulay with letter to his publishers, 1856   [T]
5 T. B. Macaulay, *The History of England*, (5 vols, 1848-61)   [UL]
6 Beatrice Lock, *Portrait of F. W. Maitland*, oil on canvas   [DOW]
7 F. W. Maitland, *History of English Law* (1895), 1968 CUP reprint of important 1898 2nd ed.
8 F. W. Maitland, *Domesday Book and Beyond* (1897), CUP reprint, 1988   [CUP]
9 *Letters of F. W. Maitland*, ed. C.H.S. Fifoot, 1965   [UL]
10 Lord Acton, *The Cambridge Modern History*, vol 1 (of 14) first published 1902; this copy 1907   [UL]
11 Bede, *Ecclesiastical History of the English People*, post-737   [UL]

17 Outreach

This section of the exhibition examines the contributions Cambridge has made, and continues to make, to the wider world. It begins with a group of items relating to *Emmanuel, Harvard, and the New World*, and beyond, and includes material on the *Cambridge University Local Examinations Syndicate,* which now has examination centres in almost every country, and the *Board of Continuing Education,* which runs lecture programmes and day and summer schools at Madingley Hall and throughout the region. Photographs show the work of Cambridge archaeologists and anthropologists in Ethopia and Nagaland.

1 Emmanuel Admissions Register, open to show the signature of John Harvard, 19 Dec 1627   [EM]
2 Letter from N. Ward to the Master of Emmanuel, written on board ship to the New World, May 1635   [EM]
3 N. Ward (pseud. Theodore de la Guard), *The Simple Cobler of Aggravvam in America*, 1647   [EM]
4 Proclamation by the Virginia Company to encourage settlement, 1620   [M]

5 Remembrances to be sent to Lord Delaware respecting his Governorship of Virginia, 1611   [M]
6 List of passengers shipped on the *James* to Virginia, 1622   [M]
7 Copy of letter sent from the Master of Emmanuel to the President of Harvard in connection with the Emmanuel Tercentenary celebrations   [EM]
8 Printed address on the Harvard Tercentenary, 1936   [EM]
9 Book of photographs of Harvard, c.1912   [UL]
10 Malcolm Osborne, *Helen Cam*, graphite on paper, 1948 (the year Cam moved from Girton to become Harvard's first woman professor)   [G]
11 T. Kendall and S. Lee, *A Grammar and Vocabulary of the Language of New Zealand*, 1820,   [UL]

Nos 12-15 have been lent by the *University of Cambridge Local Examinations Syndicate*

12 Examination papers in bound volume, 1880
13 Display shown by the Syndicate at the Paris Exhibition, 1900
14 Results Book, 1924
15 Queen's Award for Export Achievement, certificate, 1992

Nos 16-20 have been lent by the *University of Cambridge Board of Continuing Education*

16 H. von Herkomer, *Portrait of James Stuart* (unfinished), oil on canvas, late 19th cent.
17 G. Leigh-Mallory, *Modern History*, local lecture syllabus, c.1923
18 G. Leigh-Mallory, *Modern Democracy*, local lecture syllabus, c.1923
19 Advertisement for Summer meeting on *The Victorian Age*, 1928
20 Poster advertising a lecture on Cambridge University in Great Yarmouth, 1939

18 Theatre

Theatre has always been strong at Cambridge; the ADC is England's oldest university playhouse, and Footlights is the best-known of the University's theatrical clubs.

1 Arts Theatre, opening programme, 3 Feb 1936   [K]
2 Arts Theatre, programme with photographs, 17 Feb 1936   [K]
3 Keynes' family scrapbook showing the Arts Theatre opening   [K]

Nos 4-20 have been lent by the *Footlights Archive*

4 *Aladdin*, cast photograph, 1883

5 *Cheer-Oh Cambridge*, cast photograph, 1913
6 *All the Vogue*, programme for May Week revue, 1925
7 Malcolm Burgess, *A Flash in the Cam*, set design, 1951
8 Malcolm Burgess, *Tip and Run*, set design, 1952
9 *Between the Lines*, cast photograph, 1955
10 *My Girl Hubert*, cast photograph, 1965
11 *Chox*, cast photograph, 1974
12 *The New Dean*, lyric book, 1897
13 *The Freshman*, lyric book, 1902
14 *The Honorary Degree*, lyric book, 1907
15 *The 'Varsity B C'*, lyric book, 1908
16 *Cheer-Oh! Cambridge*, lyric book, 1913
17 *A Bang and a Whimper*, lyric book, 1993
18 *La Vie Cambridgienne*, poster, 1948
19 *Cinderella*, Spring revue poster, 1979
20 *Suitable Silly*, Spring revue poster, 1990

19 Music

This section displays the wealth of Cambridge's musical heritage including recent scores by A. Goehr and R. Holloway.

1 French missal, vellum, c.1200   [FM]
2 *Springfield Antiphoner*, c.1300   [UL]
3 Leaves of English church polyphony, vellum, early 14th cent.   [FM]
4 Lutebook of Christopher Lowther, c.1637   [FM]
5 Lute book, 1600   [UL]
6 Beethoven, *Opus III, Grand Sonata*, c.1823, printed score with dedication on title page   [UL]
7 A. Goehr, *The Death of Moses*, 1992
8 R. Holloway, *Clarissa*, 1990

20 Law & Politics

This section of the exhibition contains a photographic survey of famous graduates in these fields, and current research projects.

21 Education & Teaching

Cambridge's heritage lies not only on its research successes, but on its teaching. For centuries its graduates have made important contributions to society. Today it leads the league table of excellence.

1 'Castlemaine' globe, plaster of Paris on wooden pedestal, made by Joseph Moxon, 1679, and supplied to the University, 1681   [UL]
2 Receipt for above globe and instruction book for £5 12s, from J. Moxon,

May 1681, with receipt from Isaac Malden for making a glass container for it, Sept 1681 [UL]

3 J. Moxon, *Mechanick Exercises*, 1677-83 [UL]

4 Receipt for purchase of 2 volumes of the above, bought from Moxon for the University Library, 29 Aug. 1684 [UL]

5 Cabinet with a collection of geological specimens, burr walnut veneer, 1690s. One of four made to house the collections of John Woodward, and bequeathed by him to the University for teaching purposes [SM]

6 Lecture tickets admitting students to lectures by J. J. Thomson (1901), F. Darwin (1893), A. Keynes (1895), A. Marshall (1893), all with prices [G]

7 Notes on supervisions with C. S. Lewis [Mr G. B. Skelsey]

Copies of archive photographs from Girton and prints from Cambridge Central Library are also displayed

22 University Life

A variety of undergraduate life past and present is represented here, from student sport to debates at the Union Society.

1 *Gradus ad Cantabrigium; or new University Guide*, pub. J. Hearne, 1824 [UL]

2 Undergraduate dinner party, photograph, 1890s [CCL]

3 Blazer, belonging to a member of *The Lunatics* society, c. 1929 [SID]

4 Sidney Sussex cricket XI, photograph, 1924 [SID]

5 Printed ephemera relating to May Balls, 1960s and 1970s [CCL]

6 Printed ephemera relating to a large number of University societies, including both politics and sport, mainly 1960s and 1970s [CCL]

7 Rowing blades, including new cleaver blade, and presentation oars [CUBC]

8 Rowing blade used by W. G. R. M. Laurie in both the 1936 Boat Race and the 1948 Olympics, where he was a Gold medallist [Mrs Janet Hesketh]

9 Rowing four [CUBC]

10 *Cambridge University Boating Costumes*, printed leaflet, c.1875 [UL]

11 Boat Race chart 1888-1898 [Union Society]

12 P. Reinagle, *John Nicholson, Cambridge Bookseller*, oil on canvas, 1788 [UL]

Nos 13-21 have been lent by the *Cambridge Union Society*

13 Book of ex-officio members, 1893 onwards

14 Cuttings book, 1950s

15 Visitors' book, with signed posters, 1994

16 General view of the Union Society showing Jack Ashley as President

17 Ronald Reagan, Union Society photograph

18 Nehru, Union Society photograph

19 Ann Mallelieu, 1st woman president, Union Society photograph

20 Union Society group photograph including L. Brittan, J. Gummer, D. Frost, B. Levin

21 Union Society group photograph including M. Howard and K. Clark

23 Cambridge University Press

This section displays books and apparatus associated with the oldest press in the world, and looks at both its global impact (with thousands of authors worldwide) and its advances in new technology.

1 *Two Treatises of the Lord His Holie Supper*, published by Thomas Thomas, Cambridge, 1584. The first CUP book [UL]

2 John Milton, *Lycidas*, with ms corrections, 1638 [UL]

3 *The Bible*, printed by John Baskerville in his own type, 1763 [CUP]

4 R. Willis & J. W. Clark, *Architectural History of Cambridge*, vol 1, 1886 [UL]

5 Albion crown folio printing press, No. 656, 1857, with printed sheet showing the University Arms by Reynolds Stone [CUP]

6 Chaucer on CD-ROM: the opening page of a late-medieval manuscript of Chaucer's *The Wife of Bath's Prologue* - part of 'The *Canterbury Tales* Project', 1995 [CUP]

24 Taylor-Schechter Genizah Collection

The Taylor-Schechter Genizah Collection in the University Library contains 68,000 fragments of early Hebrew manuscripts, brought to Cambridge from Cairo by Dr Solomon Schechter, and given to the University in 1898.

1 Specimen of a fragment as received in Cairo [UL]

2 Autograph letter of Moses Maimonides (1135-1204) [UL]

3 Child's Hebrew primer, 10th cent. [UL]

25 Aerial Photography Department

This Department was set up in 1945 to take photographs in aid of teaching and research. It contains over 400,000 aerial

photographs, commissioned by a number of University departments and outside bodies, including archaeologists, engineers, geographers, and land economists. A slide sequence shows changes in a number of landscapes systematically photographed by the Department over many years.

26 Scott Polar Research Institute

Items from Scott's Antarctic expedition, 1912: nos 1-5 lent by the Institute

1 Packet of Bovril Pemmican

2 Tin of Huntley & Palmer biscuits

3 Tin of dried cabbage with cooking instructions

4 Candle lantern

5 Pair of snow shoes used by the pony

6 Gonville & Caius College flag taken on the expedition by Dr Edward Wilson, worked by Mrs Roberts, wife of the Master, 1912 [CAI]

27 The University Today

The first floor landing at Christie's displays the vital University of today, its international standing as a centre of excellence, its ability to work in partnership with the financial, industrial, and corporate sectors, its innovation and initiative at the forefront of research, its need to maintain and expand these areas, and finally its need to fund its future.

Key	
AA	Museum of Archaeology and Anthropology
BFBS	British & Foreign Bible Society
CAI	Gonville & Caius College
CavL	Cavendish Laboratory
CC	Corpus Christi College
CCL	Cambridge Central Library
CL	Computer Laboratory
CR	Combination Room
CUBC	Cambridge University Boat Club
CUP	Cambridge University Press
DOW	Downing College
EM	Emmanuel College
FM	Fitzwilliam Museum
G	Girton College
JE	Jesus College
JN	St John's College
K	King's College
M	Magdalene College
MRC	MRC Laboratory of Molecular Biology
N	Newnham College
OS	Old Schools
PEM	Pembroke College
SM	Sedgwick Museum
SID	Sidney Sussex College
T	Trinity College
UL	University Library
W	Whipple Museum
ZM	Zoology Museum
and other individual lenders as indicated	

Acknowledgements

CHRISTIE'S INTERNATIONAL PLC

MONUMENT TRUST

CAMBRIDGE UNIVERSITY PRESS

 Beneficial Bank PLC

The University of Cambridge and the Cambridge Foundation acknowledge with warm thanks the many University departments and colleges who have assisted with the *Foundations for the Future* exhibition. We would particularly like to thank those departments, colleges, and other organisations who have loaned material for display:

Mr Peter Ackroyd ◆ Mr Douglas Adams ◆ Department of Aerial Photography ◆ Department of Applied Mathematics and Theoretical Physics ◆ Faculty of Archaeology and Anthropology ◆ Museum of Archaeology and Anthropology ◆ Faculty of Architecture ◆ British and Foreign Bible Society ◆ Ms A. S. Byatt ◆ Cambridgeshire Collection - Cambridgeshire Libraries and Heritage Services ◆ Cambridge Union Society ◆ Cambridge University Boat Club ◆ Syndics of Cambridge University Library ◆ Syndics of Cambridge University Press ◆ Cambridge University Students' Union ◆ The Master, Fellows, and Scholars of Clare College ◆ Committee of Management, University Combination Room, The Old Schools, University of Cambridge ◆ The Master and Fellows of Christ's College ◆ The Master and Fellows of Churchill College ◆ Computer Laboratory ◆ Board of Continuing Education ◆ The Master and Fellows of Corpus Christi College ◆ Dr P. M. Dean, University of Cambridge ◆ Faculty of Divinity ◆ The Master, Fellows, and Scholars of Downing College ◆ Marshall Library, Faculty of Economics and Politics ◆ The Master and Fellows of Emmanuel College ◆ Department of Engineering ◆ University of Cambridge Estate Management and Building Service ◆ Syndics of the Fitzwilliam Museum ◆ Cambridge University Footlights Archive ◆ Department of Geography ◆ The Mistress and Fellows of Girton College ◆ The Master and Fellows of Gonville and Caius College ◆ Mrs Janet Hesketh ◆ Faculty of History ◆ Mr Ted Hughes ◆ Isaac Newton Institute for Mathematical Sciences ◆ The Master, Fellows, and Scholars of Jesus College ◆ Judge Institute of Management Studies ◆ Kettle's Yard ◆ The Provost and Fellows of King's College ◆ Faculty of Law ◆ University of Cambridge Local Examinations Syndicate ◆ The Master and Fellows of Magdalene College ◆ Department of Materials Science and Metallurgy ◆ Department of Medicine ◆ School of Clinical Medicine ◆ Medical Research Council Laboratory of Molecular Biology Cambridge ◆ Faculty of Music ◆ University Neurology Unit ◆ The Principal and Fellows of Newnham College ◆ University Registry, The Old Schools, University of Cambridge ◆ The Master and Fellows of Pembroke College ◆ Department of Pharmacology ◆ Faculty of Philosophy ◆ Department of Physics, Cavendish Laboratory ◆ Institute of Public Health ◆ Department of Pure Mathematics and Mathematical Statistics ◆ The Master and Fellows of St John's College ◆ The Master and Fellows of Queens' College ◆ Scott Polar Research Institute ◆ Sedgwick Museum, Department of Earth Sciences ◆ The Master and Fellows of Sidney Sussex College ◆ Mr Geoffrey Skelsey, University of Cambridge ◆ Research Centre in Superconductivity ◆ Department of Surgery ◆ The Master and Fellows of Trinity College ◆ The Master, Fellows, and Scholars of Trinity Hall ◆ Vice-Chancellor, University of Cambridge ◆ Whipple Museum of the History of Science ◆ Department of Zoology ◆ University Museum of Zoology

The exhibition organisers are especially grateful to the following individuals throughout the University, colleges, and other organisations, for their help:

Aerial Photography: David Newland ◆ American Friends of Cambridge University: Tamsin Palmer ◆ Archaeology and Anthropology: David Phillipson, Christopher Chippindale, Anita Herle ◆ Faculty of Architecture: Peter Carolin, Nicholas Ray ◆ Audio Visual Aids Unit: Martin Gienke, Don Manning ◆ Cambridge Central Library: Michael Petty ◆ Cambridge Evening News: Robert Satchwell, Tony Wicken ◆ Cambridge Union Society: Barry Thoday ◆ Cambridge University Boat Club: John Adamson, John Marks ◆ Cambridge University Library: Richard Andrewes, Paul Ayris, Gerry Bye, Elisabeth Leedham-Green, Adam Perkins, Stefan Reif, Jonathan Topham, Patrick Zutshi ◆ Cambridge University Press: Jeremy Mynott, William Davies, Adrian du Plessis, Geoff Staff, Kevin Taylor ◆ Cavendish Laboratory: Haroon Ahmed, John Deakin, Shirley Fieldhouse, Archie Howe, Keith Papworth ◆ Christie's International plc: Sir Anthony Tennant, Robin Hambro, Press and Events Office ◆ Faculty of Classics: Mary Beard ◆ Colebrook Consulting Ltd: Bob Hayes ◆ Computer Laboratory: Stuart Lang, Roger Needham ◆ Board of Continuing Education: Susan Rawlings, Mike Richardson ◆ Parker Library, Corpus Christi College: Gill Cannell, Nigel Wickens ◆ Development Office, especially: Mary Evans, Barbara Beckett, Catherine Bradley, Claire Briggs, Maree Carter, Carolyn Causton, Chris Hesketh, Beth Hunter, Jenny Jardine, Jo Raines ◆ Faculty of Divinity: David Ford ◆ Downing College: Philip Howell ◆ Emmanuel College: Sarah Bendell, Ruth Bruce ◆ Department of Engineering: David Newland ◆ Faculty of English: Gillian Beer, Peter Holland ◆ Estate Management and Building Services: David Todd-Jones ◆ Financial Board: Joanna Womack, Peter Mardles, Suzy Bishop ◆ Fitzwilliam Museum: Simon Jervis, Robin Crighton, David Scrase, Lesley Nolan ◆ Footlights Archive: Harry Porter ◆ Sir Norman Foster and Partners: Michael Jones ◆ General Board: David Livesey, Diane Everett ◆ Girton College: Kate Perry ◆ Hamilton Kerr Institute: Ian McClure ◆ Faculty of History: Quentin Skinner, Jonathan Shepard ◆ Isaac Newton Institute for Mathematical Sciences: Robert Harding, Peter Landshoff, Steve Leigh ◆ Judge Institute of Management Studies: Eddie Anderson ◆ Kettle's Yard: Michael Harrison, Katrina Purser ◆ King's College: Peter Jones ◆ Magdalene College: Richard Luckett ◆ Molecular Research Council Laboratory: Margaret Browne, Mike Fuller ◆ Museums & Galleries Commission: May Cassar, Brian Dovey, Gerry McQuillan, Peter Osborne, Heather Wilson ◆ Newnham College: Frances Hazlehurst, Carola Hicks ◆ Department of Pharmacology: Alan Cuthbert, Phillip Dean ◆ Faculty of Philosophy: Tom Baldwin ◆ Physical Education: Tony Lemons ◆ Publications Officer: Janet Keystone ◆ Queens' College: John Polkinghorne ◆ University Registry: Stephen Fleet, Yvonne Garrod, Mike Hughes ◆ Scott Polar Research Institute: Robert Headland ◆ Sidney Sussex College: Nick Rogers ◆ Research Centre in Superconductivity: Yao Liang ◆ Trinity College: David McKitterick ◆ Vice-Chancellor's Office: Geoffrey Skelsey, Susannah Thomas, Pauline Howard, Margaret Stevens, Julie Durrant ◆ University College London: Janet Browne ◆ Wellcome Unit, Department of History and Philosophy of Science: Mark Weatherall ◆ Wellcome Trust and Cancer Research Campaign Institute of Cancer and Developmental Biology: Ron Laskey ◆ The Wellcome Centre for Medical Science: Laurence Smaje ◆ Department of Zoology: Patrick Bateson ◆ Zoology Museum: Ken Joysey

Additional thanks are extended to all those not listed here who have made valuable contributions in helping to mount the exhibition.